# REMEMBERING
# LaGRANGE

# REMEMBERING
# LaGRANGE
## MUSINGS *from* AMERICA'S
## GREATEST LITTLE CITY

*Julia Traylor Dyar*

Charleston · London

THE
History
PRESS

Published by The History Press
Charleston, SC 29403
www.historypress.net

First published 2011

Manufactured in the United States

ISBN 978.1.60949.122.2

Library of Congress Cataloging-in-Publication Data

Dyar, Julia.
Remembering LaGrange : musings from America's greatest little city / Julia Dyar.
p. cm.
Summary: A collection of columns written from historical newspaper articles from the
LaGrange daily news.
Includes bibliographical references.
ISBN 978-1-60949-122-2
1. LaGrange (Ga.)--History--Anecdotes. 2. LaGrange (Ga.)--Social life and customs--
Anecdotes. 3. LaGrange (Ga.)--Biography--Anecdotes. I. LaGrange daily news. II. Title.
F294.L17D93 2011
975.8'463--dc22
2011000842

*This book is dedicated to the memory of the writers and staff members of LaGrange's newspapers for recording the daily, or weekly, history of LaGrange and the times, in the inimitable style of hometown newspapers everywhere; and to the memory of my great-great-grandfather, George Hamilton Traylor (1799–1869), a pioneer settler of Troup County, Georgia, and to all of his descendants for making this section of Georgia our home.*

*And, as always, to the glory of God.*

# Contents

# Acknowledgements

I would like to express my appreciation to the following people and groups of people for their time, assistance, generosity and encouragement in the production of *Remembering LaGrange*: to Chris Cleaveland for the Vintage postcards from his collection, used as illustrations in this book; to my niece Mary Ann Traylor Hudson for her generous support, her faithful and invaluable assistance in proofreading, her critique of the entire book and her suggestions that improved it; to my niece Lelia Kincaid Cort and nephew Tommy Kincaid Jr. for their skillful proofreading of many chapters; to my niece Jan Gelders-Tucker for her special interest in the project; to Daniel Baker and the staff at the *LaGrange Daily News*; to Kaye Minchew, Clark Johnson and others on the staff at the Troup County Historical Society and Archives; to Charlene Baxter and the Frank and Laura Lewis Library at LaGrange College; to Jonathan Lawson, Computer Doc & Associates; and to all my family for their steadfast love and inspiration.

Additional attribution: Some items used in the sections "Decade Reviews— Nationally" were found in *The World Book*; Time Education Program, 1901– 1965; "The American Century in Food," *Bon Appétit*; and "The Century," a special section in the *LaGrange Daily News* in 2000.

# Introduction

In 1993, after retiring from a forty-five-year-long career in newspaper journalism and college public relations, this scribe intended to enjoy a more relaxed life with family and friends—with more time for her church and favorite volunteer work in her hometown, LaGrange, Georgia.

After several months, this compulsive writer became bored and frustrated without deadlines, and she went to her friend, the late Glen Long, then publisher of the local daily newspaper, the *LaGrange Daily News*, to see if he had a part-time job she could apply for, even as a proofreader. He suggested that she give some thought to writing a column.

With her great love for writing, newspapers, history and her hometown, she thought of researching old issues of LaGrange newspapers from one hundred, seventy-five, fifty and twenty-five years ago and selecting interesting material, by month, in the designated years to prepare weekly columns. Fortunately, many of these newspapers were still available in the Troup County Archives and/or the *Daily News*'s morgue.

Her first "Memoried Glances" column was published in December 1993; the column is published weekly in the *LaGrange Daily News* and is now in its seventeenth year.

Several years before the turn of the century, this writer was asked by then editor of the newspaper, Andrea Lovejoy, to assist in collecting historical data for a special edition to be published in 2000. The data, compiled by decades at that time, has been useful in preparing this book.

This has been a rewarding journey into the captivating past of a hometown, rediscovering wonderful stories and excellent editorials revealing the intellect, vision and humor of the writers, as well as information about the men and women who have helped make LaGrange an exceptionally fine hometown.

The findings were too significant not to preserve and share in another genre. This book is the result. It is not to be considered a history per se; it is a historical chronicle offering the reader a sampling of the gleanings from a small hometown newspaper that recorded the news as it happened, weekly or daily, and that reflected in its editorials the discernment and humor of its writers.

Space limits the scope of this book. The author, or chronicler, hopes it will capture the true spirit of a great hometown in *any* year.

# Prologue

In *The History of Troup County*, published in 1933, Clifford Lewis Smith of LaGrange, the author, wrote, "The aim of the local newspapers has ever been to bring the news to their readers in an entertaining manner, to uphold the lofty principles of our government, to promote civic and urban growth, and to disseminate culture and enlightenment among the readers."

The greater part of the material recorded here from 1894 to the late 1920s came from the *LaGrange Reporter*, the *LaGrange Graphic* or the *LaGrange Graphic-Shuttle*. From 1930 forward, the *LaGrange Daily News* was the source.

In the years before the time covered in this book, LaGrange was incorporated on December 16, 1828, and named the county seat of Troup County in the same legislation. The town was named for the French estate of the Marquis de Lafayette, the Revolutionary War hero, who was greatly admired in this section of the country, and by all Americans, for his help during the Revolutionary War.

According to Mr. Smith's history of the county, "Many of the settlers were people of education and property, and they brought with them tools, cattle, slaves and household furnishings. Almost immediately they began to plan for schools and churches."

Creek Indians were living across the Chattahoochee River and were friendly at first. Later they pillaged and took cattle from the settlers and were forced to move west.

During the War Between the States (1861–1865), LaGrange had a company of female soldiers, called the Nancy Harts, organized to protect the homes and children when the men were away fighting in the war. In

In 1825, Lafayette, a Revolutionary War hero, visited Georgia and was reminded of his French estate, Chateau de LaGrange. LaGrange was named in his honor.

In April 1865, the Nancy Harts, LaGrange women's militia, marched from the Dallis home to defend the city from Yankee troops. Their bravery saved local homes.

1865, the women marched to meet Yankee raiders commanded by a Colonel LaGrange. The ladies surrendered on the colonel's promise to spare the homes from destruction.

The timeline for this book begins in 1894, after LaGrange had survived the War Between the States and was already known for its hospitable and cultured residents, its lovely old houses spared during the war, its fine cultural and religious institutions and its substantial business interests.

By 1894, LaGrange was considered an "Educational Center." It had two female colleges, LaGrange Female College and Southern Female College, and privately operated LaGrange High School for boys. It had five churches (Baptist, Episcopalian, two Methodist and Presbyterian), two newspapers and two hotels.

In 1895, the May edition of *Southern Cultivator*, according to Troup County history, described LaGrange as a "beautiful little educational and manufacturing city." It described the people as "educated, refined and progressive."

At that time the city had a fire department, waterworks and an electric light plant. Soon would follow the expansion of its strong beginnings in the textile industry. Some family names linked to the early years of the cotton mills in LaGrange were Robertson, Leslie, Park, Bigham, Truitt, Dunson and Callaway.

Selections from early newspapers offered here include human interest items and editorial commentary that reflected the editors' observations on history as it was being made and revealed life in a small Georgia hometown.

In each decade remembered, there was local newspaper coverage on front pages and on editorial pages about other news happening in the state, the nation and the world. This news also had an influence on the daily and weekly lives of LaGrange readers. Some of the important topics covered are listed in "Decade Reviews" for each ten-year period in this book after 1900, focusing on national and sometimes world events.

All the illustrations are postcards, used as a courtesy of Chris Cleaveland of LaGrange, from his collection of historic postcards. A few of them show an additional credit.

Now, let's begin in the 1890s.

## CHAPTER I

# The Decade of the 1890s

From 1894
From the *LaGrange Reporter*

The decade of the 1890s was a period of continued growth and prosperity for LaGrange. The city's future was addressed in an editorial describing its position at that time, according to the *Reporter*'s editor:

> *Our Future—For many years LaGrange has been recognized as a good, substantial town, a place of culture and refinement, one of the results of her splendid institutions of learning. Many of her citizens have possessed wealth. Creameries and other small manufacturing plants have followed in the wake of the big cotton factories. Within ten years the population of the city has doubled. We are no longer inhabitants of a sleepy, contented country town. We are living in a thriving, hustling and enterprising little city of six thousand souls.*

This was a decade for looking to the future, and the editor was, as he added: "Nothing should deter us in our determination to make LaGrange one of the best small cities in Georgia. The brains and the money are here to accomplish any undertaking, and if the inclination is not lacking, we will soon have a city of twelve thousand souls."

The "big cotton factories" received more praise in an editorial in 1898, as the editor wrote, "Two manufacturing institutions to which the people look with pride, are the LaGrange Mills (chartered as a manufacturer of cotton

Smith Hall in the late 1800s, the oldest building at LaGrange College, founded in 1831. The building was restored in 1989 and is on the National Register of Historic Places.

Southern Female College, founded in 1842. Fire destroyed buildings in 1908. After renovations, the school was forced to close in 1919 due to financial problems. The buildings were converted to apartments.

textiles in 1888) and the Dixie Cotton Mills (founded in 1895). It is gratifying that these industries, built solely by home capital, are prospering." Another prediction from the editor followed: "We predict that it is only a question of time when more of their kind will be built and the hum of many thousand spindles will pronounce LaGrange a great manufacturing center. Here's to success for our Cotton Mills!"

The "splendid institutions of learning" were addressed in a later editorial, which expressed pride in the past, as well as advice for the future, in these words: "Our Greatest Pride—If LaGrange will always take care of her schools they will take care of her. Our greatest pride has ever been in the progress and prosperity of our institutes of learning."

In a lengthy editorial the writer cited, by name, the already established LaGrange Female College, dating from 1831; the Southern Female College, founded in 1842; and Park High School for boys, built in 1895. During the 1890s, the LaGrange High School for boys also provided a quality curriculum for the young men of the city and received much praise in the *Reporter*.

"Public schools for LaGrange" was the question for discussion in the 1890s. Troup County had a public school system as early as the 1870s, but residents of LaGrange voted against the idea several times. They seemed to prefer the private schools already serving the city. An editorial, in 1894, asked a question:

> *Public Schools? After many disappointments it seems that our people have at last made up their minds to have a system of public schools. LaGrange must either "get there"—have free schools—or take her position in the rear of the procession. Are we ready to accept such an assignment by the public opinion of the state and the whole country? We think not. Then, let us take the necessary step and have a vote on the question as quickly as possible.*

Public schools were not inaugurated in LaGrange until 1903.

In 1895, the editor gave his readers some sound/unusual advice. He expressed the feelings of many true Americans in the South after the War Between the States when he wrote:

> *True To Old Glory—We think it would be a good thing if, when officials of the North and South meet, they would studiously avoid all reference to the war. Our respective opinions on that subject cannot be changed, and no amount of gush will help the matter. The South was right, from our*

*standpoint—the North, from hers. But it isn't natural to glorify the fellows who licked us back into the Union. We were forced back—and we have, like men of sense and patriotism, made the best of it. We are true to the Union and "old glory" now, but our affection will not be improved by belittling the cause for which we sacrificed everything.*

LaGrange readers could rely on the *Reporter* to inform them on state, national and world news of interest, as well as local. Some examples, all from the 1890s, begin with the final paragraph of a lengthy article on the question of voting for women, an important subject in February 1895. It quoted Mrs. W.Y. Atkinson, wife of the Georgia governor, who said: "When the women of Georgia earnestly desire to vote, the men will not stand in their way. When women feel that it is in the interest of the country that they be given the ballot, they will ask for it; should this time come in Georgia there will be as many men as women who will advocate bestowing the rights of suffrage upon them."

The right to vote was given to women in 1920.

Another national topic of importance to LaGrange readers was addressed in May 1895 on the subject of "Federal Income Taxes." The editor wrote:

*At one stroke the United States Supreme Court has swept from the statute books forever the income tax law. Henceforth taxation must fall upon the production classes. The rich, the bondholders, the real estate owners are exempt. The court's decision was a five to four opinion. The dissenting judges hinted at the prospect of bloody revolution in the future as it adds to the burdens under which the laboring people are already groaning.*

The editor's comments on world news of concern to LaGrange citizens were read with great interest, especially the editorial in February 1898 regarding the "*Maine* Disaster." It read, in part:

*Perhaps never before in the history of our nation have our anger and the passions of the American people been as stirred up as since the disaster which wrecked the United States Battleship Maine, in the Havana harbor last week, when several brave officers and two hundred and fifty sailors went down into a watery grave. The war feeling is running high all over the country.*

Indeed it was. The Spanish-American War followed in 1898. A call for troops was made in April 1898, and some members of the LaGrange Light Guards were among those volunteering for service.

Through the years, residents of LaGrange have taken pride in many things concerning the city's development and its advantages in many areas, relating to the quality of life here. In 1898, the editor mentioned another point of local pride: "LaGrange—The City of Elms and Roses—The beautiful elm trees, three thousand of which were set out on our sidewalks years ago, are now the pride of the town. In the future in welcoming guests to our city, we may all say, as did Dr. F.M. Ridley in his recent welcome to Judge Spencer R. Atkinson, 'We welcome you to the city of elms and roses.'"

## Mosaic Musings from the 1890s

*One of the crying needs of Georgia is a State Reformatory where juvenile criminals may be trained out of vicious courses into useful and honorable citizenship. A timely expenditure now, in that direction, will save the state a much heavier cost in the future when they have graduated in crime.*

*The Legislature has decided to establish a State Board of Medical Examiners. This has been a crying need and it will save the people from being so greatly imposed upon by half-educated humbugs and quacks.*

*Mr. J.W. O'Berry has just finished for Dr. Enoch Callaway a handsome, closed-top physician's phaeton, which is certainly one of the most creditable jobs ever issued from any carriage works. It is elegant, strong, luxuriously comfortable and stylish.*

*Mr. Wade Milam, manager and proprietor of our local telephone system, informs us that already he has put in seventy new telephones, with more to be placed as soon as they come. This surely goes a long way toward making a good impression of our city in the minds of visitors. You can say "hello" to your neighbor, your grocer, your doctor or anyone else who has a wire connecting them with "central," for only $1.50 per month.*

*The "bike craze" is growing in LaGrange. A great many wheel-men can be seen every afternoon and night enjoying the fascinating sport. Bicycle riders should read the notice in today's paper that says, "No riding will be allowed on the sidewalks hereafter."*

# WINSOME MURMURS FROM THE 1890s

*Our friend, Mr. Toad Henderson, thinks that those who have hens to dispose of should hold them a while longer, for present omens indicate that they are "going up." He has one that has "gone up" into a huge oak tree to the height of forty feet, where she is now serenely engaged in the work of incubation.*

*It is said that the banks in the county are gaining currency as fast as an unfounded rumor.*

*Now a woman wants Congress to pass a bill to make men marry. The old maids are giving the bill their hearty support.*

*The Presbyterians are very much opposed to women in the pulpit. They are right.*

*LaGrange should have an automobile. Who will be the first one to purchase?*

*Those fond of angling will not be compelled to hie themselves to the country streams. Good fishing may be had on the Square in LaGrange, but mud cats will be in the ascendancy.*

*Train up a child in the way he should go and the first thing you know he is gone.*

*Women ought to make good legislators. Many a man can testify that a woman's word is law.*

## CHAPTER 2

# Turn of the Century
## *The 1900s*

From *LaGrange Reporter*

R esidents of LaGrange found the turn of the new century, the 1900s, an exciting time, filled with hope and the promise of even greater growth.

The *LaGrange Reporter*, a weekly newspaper for more than fifty years, was now a daily. LaGrange residents—on a daily basis—were reading more about their wider world. At home, many new homes were being built all over town.

As early as 1902, local folks were talking about "the automobile"; in fact, the entire decade of the 1900s brought occasional news and editorial items on the automobile's late acceptance by LaGrange prospective buyers, who were, as the newspaper described them, "noted for their wise conservatism."

In 1902, and again in 1904, an Atlanta man representing a dealer for Oldsmobiles drove to LaGrange to demonstrate the latest models. He took a few "fearless citizens automobiling," according to the *Reporter*, including some young ladies—"who were not afraid." The model he brought in 1902 cost $950.

The representative's route to LaGrange brought him through Newnan, giving its residents their first view of an automobile. "The run from Atlanta to Newnan," according to the *Reporter*, "was made in three hours." This was a distance of less than forty miles.

In 1904, it was reported that "the Oldsmobile representative has made sales of several machines in LaGrange, one just delivered to Mr. T.J. Thornton." At that time, several local doctors were contemplating using automobiles in their practices.

Main Street Scene. Card postmarked 1906. Elmrose Hotel, later the LaGrange Hotel, burned in 1931. Truitt Opera House is on left.

In 1906, the Georgia legislature was preparing to pass a law "regulating the running of automobiles in the state." The *Reporter*, in an editorial in the summer of that year, explained: "One member of that august body wants the law to give citizens the right to shoot when automobiles are run on the public highways; while another wants the law to prohibit the running of the machines except through the woods."

By May 1907, the newspaper reported that "LaGrange has made a few purchases of automobiles," which could explain the headline, "A Speed Limit," that followed in June. The news item stated that the city had passed an ordinance regulating the "speed of automobiles on the streets of LaGrange. The city authorities think a speed of eight miles an hour is about right and will do away with all danger."

Horse-drawn vehicles were still needed in LaGrange for day-to-day travel, as well as some special occasions, such as weddings and funerals.

Two young LaGrange people were united in marriage in a buggy in March 1902. Their parents thought they were too young to marry, according to the newspaper, so the pair "eloped in a buggy and were married in haste by an understanding clergyman, the Reverend R.M. Dixon." The end of the story—"The parents have forgiven them, and the young couple are now all smiles."

In 1904, LaGrange had a new rubber-tired white hearse, described by the *Reporter* as "one of the handsomest ever seen in this section. It was drawn by a beautiful pair of gray horses."

Beginning in January 1901 the *Reporter* was expressing the pride of all LaGrange citizens in the "new buildings being constructed in every part of the city." LaGrange was enjoying a "building boom" of handsome residences and cottages, as well as the almost completed building of the Unity Cotton Mills, expected to be ready about the first of November.

The newspaper, in February 1901, was continuing to express concern on its editorial page over the city's failure to establish public schools, when the editor wrote: "Nothing adds so materially to the continued growth of the town as public schools. It is an acknowledged fact that many families contemplating moving here have gone elsewhere because we could not offer them the free facilities to educate their children."

In December 1902, "an overwhelming vote for public schools was recorded, with only three votes against it," as LaGrange citizens read in an editorial in the *Reporter*. In this same editorial, the newspaper reported that the three greatest news events of the year locally were: "the organization of a board of trade, the new sewerage system and the public school system." The editor continued to lament "the county's failure to vote bonds for a new courthouse building."

By October 1903, two new public school buildings had been completed, and the public school system in LaGrange "closed the year in 1904 with 900 pupils enrolled," a story in the *Reporter* stated.

A front-page story in March 1904 brought more good news for city and county residents as they read in the headlines of the *Reporter*, "Troup County to Have New Temple of Justice." The story continued: "The new courthouse building will take the place of the ram-shack of a building in which court has been held for the past half-century or more. It will be built at once and will cost about $50,000. The people will vote now on the way to raise the money."

In April, the election result was reported—"There were over 200 votes over the necessary two-thirds required for bonds for the new courthouse, meaning no direct taxation will be necessary."

"Downtown street paving began in 1906, using vitrified brick," the newspaper reported, "and sidewalks were paved around the Square in 1907."

In the 1900s, LaGrange had three railroad depots. *Left to right*: Macon & Birmingham, Atlanta & West Point and Atlanta, Birmingham and Atlantic Coastline.

Confederate Monument unveiled on Court Square, 1902. It was a project of the LaGrange Chapter of the United Daughters of the Confederacy.

Progress for LaGrange was "on a roll" when, in March 1906, the Atlanta, Birmingham and Atlantic Coastline Railroad signed contracts for further expansion into this section of Georgia. At that time the *Reporter*'s editor wrote: "The dreams of LaGrange's best people are being realized with a rapidity that is soon to bring this growing manufacturing city to the foremost front of the business world of the South, as it now stands at the front as a manufacturing center for this entire section."

Continued work by many local leaders who promoted this expansion brought this news in December 1906: "Tracks are being laid through our city."

Of great satisfaction to the ladies of LaGrange, in the early 1900s, was the news that the Confederate Memorial statue, sponsored by the local chapter of the United Daughters of the Confederacy, had been placed on the square during the Eighth Annual State Convention of the Georgia Division of the United Daughters of the Confederacy. The local chapter members were hostesses to other state daughters, according to the *Reporter*'s coverage of this event.

News from the Negro community often received front-page space and the support of the newspaper for their civic and religious activities. Excerpts from items published in 1900 and 1904, respectively, follow:

> *Saw Mill Running—The saw mill built by the Mutual Aid Society, a Negro organization with headquarters in LaGrange, has gone to sawing lumber for a manufacturing plant. Plans now are to build a coffin factory and later a cotton mill. This is a commendable move and it is hoped that they will push their industries forward to completion.*

> *Annual Negro Conference—Professor R.G. Robinson, principal of the LaGrange Academy (a Methodist-related Negro school that came into the public school system in 1903), has scheduled a conference of colored people to convene in LaGrange to be known as the Annual Negro Conference. Object of the convention is to encourage Negroes to buy land, own stock, educate their children and lay aside the credit system. All white people are cordially invited to be present.*

The meeting was held in February 1901 and drew many well-known people, according to a further report in the *Reporter*. The 1904 item follows:

*Negroes Will Have Paper—Commencing in May a four-page, six-column newspaper will be published in LaGrange every Saturday morning by and for the colored people. It will be known as the LaGrange Advocate, and will, no doubt, be a big success from the beginning, as there is a splendid field for a Negro publication in this county. Its editors are D. Julius Fleming and A.A. Thomas; associate editors, Dr. I.T. Epps and C.H. Kelly; and business manager, A.T. Robinson.*

In January 1901, the *Reporter* carried a story that was reported after the local health authorities had a handle on the threat of a smallpox epidemic. The story read as follows:

*The Small Pox—Several weeks ago a man accompanied by his wife and child, all of whom were traveling in a wagon, made their appearance in LaGrange and it was discovered by the authorities that the man had the smallpox. The family was immediately sent to the pest house and all three had the disease. In the meantime, two other cases developed and they were sent to the pest house, the best treatment and medical skill being accorded the victims of the disease. City authorities took steps immediately to prevent the spread of the disease, and physicians have made a house to house canvass of the infected districts and vaccinated everyone. There is only one case in the pest house at present and it is thought that there will be no further spread of the disease. The city's authorities deserve credit for the splendid manner in which they have handled the matter and the steps they have taken to protect the health of the people of this city.*

Because of this smallpox threat in LaGrange, West Point quarantined against LaGrange, according to a news story that appeared in the *Reporter*. West Point officials later lifted the quarantine, and LaGrange residents were told at that time, "All who now wish to do so may visit West Point by the river without being molested by quarantine officers."

Exactly a year later, in January 1902, LaGrange readers were encouraged to read in the *Reporter* that there was no longer any danger of smallpox in LaGrange. However, the paper reported:

*All through the North and West smallpox is prevailing. Big, little, old and young in the Gate City, Atlanta, have been or will be vaccinated. There is only one case in Hogansville, the nearest point to LaGrange the disease is known to be. In LaGrange we feel very secure. Under Mayor Harwell's administration, about everybody here was vaccinated. If all the towns take hold of the vaccination question as vigorously and thoroughly as did LaGrange, the disease would soon be stamped out in all parts of the country.*

As early as 1900, LaGrange readers were finding many front-page stories and editorial references in the *Reporter* about temperance and "blind tigers," the places that were selling intoxicants illegally. One such reference, in a news story, had this headline—"To Fight Blind Tigers." The report went on, "The Reverend A.J. Moncrief, pastor of the First Baptist Church, has for several weeks been preaching a series of able sermons on the liquor traffic, and steps are now being taken to fight the sale of whiskey in the city of LaGrange. For that purpose a mass meeting of the citizens of LaGrange has been called."

The people were urged to be present at that meeting where a prohibition league was to be organized. The story concluded: "A determined effort will now be made to drive the 'blind tigers' out of the city. Everyone interested in the cause of prohibition is cordially invited to be present at this important meeting."

In January 1904, the editor appealed to the women of the community in "Temperance Notes," entreating local mothers, "for the sake of their daughters, as well as their sons, to banish intoxicating punch bowls from their entertainments." The editor appealed to the women of LaGrange not to serve "punch" at any of their social functions and urged "the Christian women and young ladies of the town to avoid the appearance of evil and cease calling the delicious drink made of fruits 'punch.' The name," he said, "was misleading." Then he asked this question: "Cannot some bright LaGrange woman give a name to this fruit drink that will be so catchy and appropriate that it will be adopted not only in our town, but will become the correct name everywhere? Cannot our hostesses call it 'nectar' until someone discovers a better name?"

During Hoke Smith's first term as governor of Georgia in 1907, the editor of the *Reporter* referred to the temperance question again when he observed that "judging from the tone of newspapers from all sections of the state, the people have made up their minds to give prohibition a fair trial after the first of January next. In every village, town and city, there are going to be efforts to operate 'blind tigers.' Judges of the Superior Courts have already given notice that offenders will be shown no mercy in the courts. The punishment should not be in the shape of fines, but in the shape of imprisonment at hard labor. That is about the only treatment that will break up the 'blind tiger' habit," he concluded.

In January 1908, a front-page story reported on the progress of acceptance of the prohibition laws in LaGrange, and the story included these observations:

> *The state prohibition law seems to be working. LaGrange was always noted for the sobriety of its citizens, but still a few would occasionally indulge in a "drop too much." Under the old order of things, a tipsy individual could be seen walking on the streets, but the vigilance of the police made that a little too expensive. Since the new law has gone into effect in Georgia, we have not seen a single individual noticeably under the influence of whiskey. That is a splendid record for even so sober a town as LaGrange.*

Immigration was a subject of great interest in LaGrange and in Troup County in this decade. A medley of editorial thoughts from the *Reporter* on this topic follows:

> *Foreigners Expected—Immigration is starting this way. Troup County farmers should begin to make ready to get their share of the foreign immigrants that are being turned in this direction. There is entirely too much uncultivated land in Troup County all for the want of labor. Foreigners will be coming in great hordes to our state and we will get some of them. Troup County should be up and doing to get the pick of the very best. Ours is the best section of the South and we should have the best class of people to settle here that are headed this way.*

Immigration of another sort was reported in a later issue, when the *Reporter* announced the arrival of some interesting four-legged "immigrants," as follows:

> *An Arrival from the North—A shipment of Boston terrier pups, that ultra fashionable breed of dogs which are so ugly that they are simply charming as pets, arrived in LaGrange last week and are now at the homes of various owners. These pups are short of tail, but long of pedigree, being from the most exclusive families of the breed. They came from away up at Rutland, Vermont, and after a week's journey by express, seemed glad to frolic about the courthouse yard and get out of Yankee land into Dixie.*

# MOSAIC MUSINGS FROM THE 1900s

*The Square and other important thoroughfares of LaGrange are in a "fix" this week. The Reporter has not been able to devise any mechanical contrivances by which one may cross the streets without wading through the deep mud. If it rains much longer there may be an opening for a ferry boat line. The mayor and council should consider paving the Square.*

*This evening at the residence of Mr. and Mrs. Fuller Callaway, there will be a "birthday party" given under the auspices of the Sunshine Band. All who attend are requested to take just as many pennies as they are old. The contributions will be used to alleviate the suffering of the poor and sick during the Christmas holidays. This band was organized several months ago by Mrs. Fuller Callaway, who is always ready to assist in any good work.*

*The pretty girl students of the LaGrange Female College enjoyed a delightful buggy ride Monday evening. To take 177 young ladies, and such lovely ones, to ride in one evening is a new idea and one that could originate only in the clever brain of Mr. C.T. Freeman. Some 30 or 40 people agreed to help Mr. Freeman provide as many teams as were necessary to give the young ladies a drive over the city. Every student of the college was in the procession that formed at the college and drove down to the Square. The clever firm of Bradfield Drug Company had arranged a "set up" for each of the fair students before the tour.*

*We understand that one of our leading businessmen now has to slip in at the back door of his home and eat his meals in the kitchen. This is the case because he told his wife one night this week about having been summoned before the grand jury and questioned about his knowledge of gambling, stating that all he knew was that the ladies' clubs in the city did a little "side gambling" now and then in playing for shirt waists, etc. He says it is tough living these days, but the truth had to be told.*

*That unearthly noise that awakens the citizens of LaGrange at a very early hour every morning, a noise which sounds like the wail of evil spirits and a cat fight mixed, which splits the air like a boy's "zooner," only on a larger scale, is the new whistle of the Troup Company's guano factory. It is so nerve-racking and spooky, suggesting that the "goblins will get you if you don't watch out," that one or two, and maybe more, citizens who had relapsed and fallen off the water wagon since making their New Year resolutions, have crawled back and now are occupying comfortable seats on that vehicle again. That whistle splits the air like a knife and sounds like it comes from around the corner, though it may be miles away from the hearer.*

*The political discussion between our citizens on the gubernatorial situation waxes very warm sometimes, but it is a good-natured warmth that is commendable. Some of these discussions are rich, rare and racy, but insofar as we have been informed, no feelings have yet been hurt or a vote changed.*

## FOUNDINGS/FIRSTS/HAPPENINGS

Confederate Monument on Court Square unveiled, project of local chapter, United Daughters of the Confederacy, 1902; Elks Lodge No. 1084, 1907; LaGrange Woman's Club, 1908; joined Georgia Federation in 1909; Young Men's Brass Band, 1908; LaGrange Elks Club, 1909

Some "firsts" in this decade—private hospital, founded by Dr. H.R. Slack, 1902; Coca-Cola Bottling, 1903; paid fire department, 1908; free mail delivery, 1908

Slack Sanitarium, private hospital, built 1902. The building later became a hotel and then became Dunson Hospital, LaGrange's first public hospital, in 1916.

# 1900s Decade Review—Nationally

President William McKinley shot by anarchist, died eight days later, 1901; Theodore Roosevelt sworn in as president, 1901; radio signals sent across Atlantic Ocean by Marconi, 1901; first airplane flight by Wright brothers, 1903; treaty signed by United States and Panama to build Panama Canal, 1903; ice cream, hamburgers and iced tea introduced at St. Louis Fair, 1904; first Mother's Day celebrated in Philadelphia, 1907; Henry Ford introduced Model T car, 1908; first regular radio broadcasts, 1909

# Winsome Murmurs from the 1900s

*The trustees of the University of Georgia have wisely decided that women cannot be admitted to the University of Georgia on the co-educational plan without legislative enactment.*

*If there is a place on earth where the streets need paving that place is LaGrange. The sight of the mud would make a pessimist of the most optimistic Georgia mule that happened to have a look.*

*It is said that an elderly lady from the county called at Morgan and Evans drug store in LaGrange the other day and asked for "some of the Monroe doctorin" which she had heard so much about. It was Mr. Evans who replied that they were "just out."*

*When we read of the divorce and domestic infelicities of the rich Northern and Western people we just cannot help being thankful that we are all Georgia crackers down this way.*

*The unhappiest woman in the world is the one with a secret that nobody wants to know.*

*Some husbands do almost anything to make their wives unspeakably happy.*

*While presents crowd the stockings and young faces grow bright, papa's pocketbook resembles more and more a mattress on which Jumbo might have slept.*

*The Georgia legislature will adjourn tonight [December 12, 1902]. Praise God from whom all blessings flow.*

*Everyone who was fortunate enough to have new clothes wore them last Sunday [Easter]. Some of us resurrected our old "jim-swingers" of the vintage of 1895 and 1896, and boldly paraded with the dressed-up folks.*

*Every galoot in LaGrange who happens to be the possessor of a revolver feels called upon to "shoot off his gun" when there is a fire alarm. If good citizens would only act as witnesses and report these violators of the law, the practice could easily be broken up.*

*Hog killing time has come to our part of Georgia, and the good eating the farmers are having with tables laden with backbone, spareribs and chitterlings is another proof that this is the best country in the world. The Thanksgiving turkey is not in the same class with the good things of hog killing time.*

*On Wednesday, a lone turkey escaped from its owner somewhere and made its way into the Bradfield Drug Company store. When the door was opened, he walked in and took up a position in a cozy corner, seemingly well satisfied to find such comfortable shelter from the bitter cold rain that was falling at the time. He absolutely refused to be interviewed as to whence he came or whither he was bound, and it is only supposed that he came to town to be in time for the Thanksgiving Day dinner.*

*The fellow who gets drunk this Christmas and shoots his gun and his profanity off along the public highways should be hauled before the grand jury and made to pay for his fun. The law is ample to protect decent folks, and they should see to its enforcement.*

*On Saturday last, the county commissioners gave the convicts of the county a holiday! They gave a barbecue dinner, and the convicts enjoyed the day in singing, dancing and other amusements.*

*The Supreme Court of Georgia has ruled that your wife has the right to pull the cover off of you on a cold winter night, and you cannot receive a divorce for thus being treated.*

*It is to be hoped that the "partisan fires" which are said to be blazing in the halls of Congress will consume the chaff that seems to be abundant there, and that the Congressmen will get down to work.*

*There was considerable excitement on the Square last Saturday morning caused by a cow brought to town by Mr. Jim Freeman. The cow showed quite an objection to being delivered to the butcher, and chased everything in sight, from the Negroes who held the ropes tied to her head and foot, to everyone who came near her on the sidewalk or in the street. Breaking loose, she came near running into several stores, scattering pedestrians in every direction before being caught.*

# CHAPTER 3
# The 1910s

From *LaGrange Reporter* and *LaGrange Graphic*

The first years of the 1910s decade were rather like the 1900s in LaGrange and the county. There were more businesses opening in town and more mills being chartered and built.

Automobiles were in the news again, but horses and bicycles were still seen on city streets. Two items in different 1910 issues of the *Reporter* were read with special interest.

In March 1911, a news report announced that Chief Reed of the LaGrange Police Department had bought two new bicycles for use by the local police force. The force was not to be increased at that time, but "by adding the bicycles the policemen will be able to give quicker and better service than they have ever done. Chief Reed says that it is his intention to give LaGrange the best police force to be found anywhere in a city of the size of LaGrange."

The second story, in September 1910, on the "Exciting Runaway" of a black horse belonging to Mr. George Brazill, read as follows:

> *The black horse of Mr. George Brazill was so badly frightened by an automobile Tuesday morning that he did not take time to see where he was going and ran into Davidson's Pharmacy. He was hitched to an empty racing cart from which he broke loose as he entered the door of the drug store. The screen doors were knocked down as the horse plunged against them, carrying them inside with him. He ran over tables and chairs until*

LaGrange Police Department. Chief F.T. Reed is seated in center. The force had seven
policemen and seven bicycles.

*he reached the prescription counter in the rear of the store where he stood
trembling until someone caught him by the bridle. It was ten minutes before
he could be quieted and brought out, during which time quite a crowd had
collected around the entrance to the store. The damage was something like
ten dollars, only the doors and one or two show cases were injured.*

A more important issue for LaGrange drivers came in that same month
when the newspaper reported that the Troup County commissioners had
called for a bond election to build and improve the public roads and bridges
in the county. The election was to be held on November 8.

The results of the election were reported on November 11, when the
headline read "Reporter Readers Will Live to See the Wisdom of the Step
Taken Tuesday." The commissioners received their authorization from
county voters to issue bonds in the amount of $200,000 for the "purpose of
improving our public roads and bridges."

Other important events were being reported early in the decade, such as
the dedication of the first new building in many years on the campus of
LaGrange Female College. In 1911, the Harriet Hawkes Memorial Hall,

an imposing four-story brick building, was dedicated. This was especially welcome news for the students, because the building offered greater space for classrooms, a larger library and even an indoor swimming pool.

In 1911, plans were being made for a new and long-awaited post office building to be built on Main Street. In that same year, the contract was let for the handsome home of textile giant Fuller E. Callaway. Both events were noted in the *Reporter*. Mr. Callaway had bought "Ferrell's Garden in December, 1911, an estate with formal flower gardens and about 90 acres of land adjoining," according to the *Reporter*. The house was completed in 1916. The new post office building was completed in 1913.

"Hills and Dales," as the Callaway estate has been known through the years, is faithfully maintained by the descendants of the Callaways and is revered by the entire community. In 2010, the Hills and Dales Estate is a "historic property of Fuller E. Callaway Foundation."

Thoughts and concern about the world situation became more troubling to LaGrange residents as war clouds were gathering relatively fast in Europe, beginning there in 1914. The sinking of the British liner the *Lusitania* by the Germans in 1915 brought sorrow and righteous indignation to LaGrange residents and to all Americans, magnified by the loss of the lives of many Americans on board.

LaGrange Post Office, completed on Main Street, 1913. In its history, the post office has had five sites. This building was razed in 2005.

# Musings from America's Greatest Little City

Our research source changes here to the *LaGrange Graphic*. For the remainder of this decade, all news and editorial commentary will be from the *Graphic*.

It was interesting to read, as LaGrange readers had done, an expression of the editor's opinion in the February 8, 1917 issue of the *Graphic*:

> *War Not Necessary—Should the United States declare war on Germany it would not be long until the South American republics would do likewise, and such a move would, in all probability, involve the entire world into this great conflict. War with Germany is not at all necessary. And we trust that Mr. Wilson, who has been lauded to such a great extent for having "kept us our of war," will so steer the affairs by which we are now confronted that he will still keep us out of the war.*

How quickly the editor's attitude had changed when on June 21, 1917, he wrote: "The die is cast, and today we are at war with Germany. No time now to theorize, but we have got to throw ourselves into the great conflict and do our part like valiant men and women. For how long, no one knows."

The editor knew this community well, for Troup County's draft exceeded its quota on the first day. A Red Cross chapter was established in LaGrange enlisting many volunteers for various projects to assist our troops at home and abroad. Troup County was "the first county in the nation to oversubscribe in all War Bond drives," according to the *Graphic*.

Many of the editorials written in 1917 are too good not to share. One, with words of warning, is an example:

> *Our country is at war with Germany good and proper; but there are a great many people who have never realized this fact. It seems that even the authorities did not realize the seriousness of the situation until it was a demonstrable fact that every movement of our army and navy was known to the imperial German government. That our country is swarming with German spies cannot be denied. This does not mean that every person who is opposed to the war is a spy. We believe that there are men who are opposed to the war, and who are opposed to conscription, that would pour out the last drop of blood in defense of this country. But there are those who are actively engaged in a secret propaganda to give aid and succor to the enemy. A strict watch should be kept over every suspect, and nothing should be left undone to apprehend and interne every one who is aiding the enemy.*

And another, written about the same time, calling for "Conscription of Everything," read:

> *We were opposed to the entry of the United States into this World War, believing that peace could be obtained by some honorable means and the awful consequences which would come to us as a nation could be averted. But we are now in the war, and our leading men make the statement that it will take all the available resources of the nation to win a victory. We believe this statement is true, and we believe that the administration should work upon this idea and conscript every man who is able to work, conscript every dollar in the nation, conscript every manufacturing industry and all other enterprises and push the war to a speedy termination. We have all the necessary resources. Put everything and everybody on a war footing and we will soon whip the fight and have a world peace.*

The account of a Red Cross rally, published in a June 1917 issue of the *Graphic*, demonstrates the patriotic spirit of LaGrange citizens at that time. The newspaper reported that "on the public Square on Monday night, the largest demonstration meeting ever held in LaGrange, brought a crowd that was organized into Divisions; each division having a commander and aide. There were a division of whites and a division of Negroes."

The story further reported, "The procession was nearly a mile long, composed of nearly 2,000 men, women and children, who marched to the strains of music furnished by the West Point Band." The purpose of the rally was to promote the work of the local Red Cross effort and enlist others in the county to join in the work. The story ended with this observation: "On the Square there were between 6,000 and 8,000 people; and during the entire time of the meeting there was no disturbance of any kind. This marks an epoch in the history of Troup County and demonstrates to the world what our people can, and will do when occasions demand."

After this rally in June, a front-page story in the *Graphic* in July brought a tribute to the "Negroes" the editor had mentioned in the rally story, stating that "the colored people of LaGrange are to be congratulated on the part taken by them in contributing to the Red Cross Fund. LaGrange is proud of the fact that she has the best class of colored citizens to be found in the South and they have the respect and confidence of the entire city."

In October 1917, the editor of the *Graphic* was asking, "Is Peace in Sight?" when he wrote:

*This question is being asked more at this time than at any time since the great conflict was precipitated in Europe more than three years ago. To answer this question definitely would necessitate a deeper insight into the future than this writer possesses. And still, we are forced to admit that we are inclined to think the peace is not far off. We have seen that what the allies have gained is more than offset by what the army of the central powers has gained. To us it seems as if the conflict has been merely a draw all the while. Notwithstanding this, the world is disgusted with the destruction of life and property and stands with uplifted hands, crying out for a cessation of murder and rapine. The world is sick of the tremendous slaughter of humanity and calls in all of its psychological power for peace; and it is because of these things that we are forced to believe that peace is not far off. Jehovah will, ere long, take a hand, and by the thunder of His awful majesty, bring this fearful carnage to a speedy end. We believe that peace is in sight.*

All LaGrange and county residents grieved, with his family, when the *Graphic* reported in November 1917 the death of Sergeant Baxter L. Schaub, the first Troup County victim of World War I. He died in a fire at Camp Wheeler and was buried in LaGrange after a military funeral in Macon, as well as a funeral service, with military honors, in LaGrange.

Sergeant Schaub had previously seen service "on the Mexican border as a member of the Fifth Infantry, National Guard of Georgia," as reported in the *History of Troup County* by Clifford Smith. He had remained in the unit when this regiment was mustered into service as the 122nd Infantry after war was declared with Germany.

Coverage of the war itself continued to dominate the news, both on the front and editorial pages of the *Graphic*. Excerpts from an editorial on February 7, 1918, read as follows:

*The American Expeditionary forces in France have already been attacked by the Germans and our own flesh and blood have been killed and wounded. The fight is on. The war is now at our own doors and we must win. There is a work for every American, and that work should be entered into whole-heartedly. Too many of our people are still asleep to the true situation. It is time to wake up. We are in the fight until we win the victory. Now let us not ask how long, but let us determine as to how soon it shall be accomplished.*

Two months later, in April 1918, came this rousing message from the editor in these words:

> *The civilized forces of Europe and America are now engaged in the most titanic struggle the world has ever known. It is a struggle between German "Kultur" on one side seeking to establish Prussianism throughout the world and Christian civilization on the other side, seeking to establish freedom of thought, and the doctrine that all men are born free and equal, and that "might does not make right." Today America is roused as she has never been before. The "Spirit of Seventy-Six" is abroad in the land, and worthy sons of noble sires are determined that Democracy shall triumph.*

By September 12, 1918, the Allies were making greater progress in the course of the war, as this editorial commentary reflects: "The war news grows better and better from day to day. Our allies are pushing the Germans right back to their territory, and when they are forced to fight on German soil you may expect for them to holler 'Kamerad.' With the low morale of the soldiers, it would not be surprising if the German army should collapse."

The very next week, the *Graphic*'s editor was ready to dictate the terms of the peace himself. His suggestion was "unconditional surrender of the Armies and Navies; the death penalty for the Kaiser and every military and political leader responsible for bringing on this terrible war, as the only terms upon which peace should be entered into with Germany."

On October 17, 1918, Secretary of War Baker announced that "2,008,931 American soldiers are overseas and our losses are exceedingly small considering the size of the forces transported."

In the last October issue of the *Graphic* on October 31, citizens of LaGrange and the county were concerned to read this front-page headline: "Influenza Rapidly Increasing in City." The newspaper reported more information about the growing threat of the epidemic of influenza rapidly on the increase in the city.

Dr. Clyde Givens, chairman of the LaGrange Board of Health, had urged that all children be kept off the streets and that all precautions be taken to hinder the spread of the disease. At that time, according to the newspaper report, "the epidemic seems to be worse in the mill districts in town, and unless the disease is checked, the manufacturing plants will be handicapped for lack of operatives." The report concluded with the observation that "very few deaths have occurred from the epidemic."

That situation had changed by November 7, when the *Graphic* reported, "Open air funerals only should be held in LaGrange at the request of city authorities," adding that "it was becoming almost impossible to get medical service as under normal conditions."

The next big news about the progress of the war came when the *Graphic* announced, "November 11, 1918, will go down as the greatest and most momentous day in the history of the world."

The newspaper further reported that as soon as word was received here that the war was over, "whistles were blown, bells were rung and automobiles honked as never before. The fire truck was brought out and it dashed around the city like wild, and exploded at every few intervals."

The story added that "a parade was held at 2 p.m., beginning on Main street, led by bearers of American, English and French flags. In the procession, the Hillside and Unity Spinning Mill bands came next, followed by the local Boy Scout troops and Callaway Department Store employees, who carried umbrellas made of American flags. Patriotic floats followed to the cheering of a joyful 'mass of humanity' that had filled the streets before one o'clock." The report concluded: "For several hours the crowd remained downtown, extremely happy and grateful to our all-wise God that once more peace has succeeded war; with everyone hopeful that never again will the nations of the world be forced to pass through another ordeal as it has been forced to pass through during the last four years."

By November 21, 1918, the *Graphic* was reporting that the influenza situation was greatly improved, and tributes were being paid to the medical heroes of the epidemic—the local doctors, nurses and the Red Cross, as well as many doctors and nurses from other towns who had come to help in the emergency.

After the war was over, when LaGrange and Troup County soldiers returned home, they found that an Employment Bureau had been established in LaGrange to help them find work if their jobs had not been held for them. They also found a community of grateful friends and relatives happy to welcome them home and back into the life of the community. An American Legion post had been organized, named for Sergeant Baxter Schaub, the first Troup County victim of the war.

The final count of those in the armed forces from LaGrange and Troup County who lost their lives in World War I, as listed in *The History of Troup County*, numbered "25 White Soldiers who died in service" and "18 Colored Soldiers who died in service."

The Hills and Dales villa was completed in 1916, home of LaGrange textile magnate Fuller E. Callaway. *Courtesy of Hills and Dales Estate, Historic Project, Fuller E. Callaway Foundation.*

A new hope was stirring in the hearts of LaGrange residents at the end of the decade of the 1910s. The war was over and the influenza epidemic had subsided.

With pride, local citizens read in the *Graphic* in August 1919 that one of their own highly respected and well-loved citizens, Fuller E. Callaway, had been "in France and had witnessed the signing of the peace treaty at Versailles on June 28."

Mr. Callaway had returned to LaGrange in August after several months in Europe, where he had represented the National Association of Cotton Manufacturers, of which he was chairman. The group had commissioned him to invite foreign participation in a World Cotton Conference to be held in New Orleans in October of that year.

The newspaper story concluded with, "Mr. Callaway succeeded in arranging for the European delegates to the Cotton Conference to stop in LaGrange en route to New Orleans for a Southern barbecue and other entertainment at Hills and Dales."

## MOSAIC MUSINGS FROM THE 1910S

*Perhaps nearly every man in LaGrange "trembled in his boots" this week when the local millinery shops displayed their new fall hats. Later his pocket book will receive the shock. But all this is expected, like the rumblings of Vesuvius, and one soon forgets the disturbance until the next time. We understand the displays are the most elaborate of many seasons, and the ladies have had a feast all week.*

*The straw hat is no more this year. The date for laying it aside was September 15, and if you persist in wearing yours now, there are many eyes gazing at you when you walk down the streets in LaGrange.*

*We are facing a season of dressy young men. They are stepping out of uniform into brand new clothes with flash and snap. The marrying parsons ought to do a good business this spring.*

*Uncle Sam is a queer old character. After the Armistice was signed the slogan was "Buy, Buy, and Keep the Wheels of All Industries Moving." Now the slogan is "Practice Thrift and Economy and Reduce the High Cost of Living." If Uncle Sam would practice a little more economy, he could, with more consistency, insist upon economy for his children.*

*The smartest cow in LaGrange is at 24 Main street. When she is thirsty, she goes to the hydrant and turns on the water and helps herself. She has not yet learned to turn it off, but will do so soon, since she has an investigative mind. After drinking she gazes at the flow of water as if it was a great mystery that the water will not cease. This cow belongs to Mrs. H.D. Floyd.*

*Attention Ladies—If a young lady will take a course of shorthand at Southern Business College in Atlanta, she will be independent; she need not marry unless she wants to, and if she does marry she can support her husband. Send today for a catalogue.*

## OPENINGS/FOUNDINGS

First local airfield, 1910; Dunson Mills chartered, 1910; Ideal Theater, 1912; Hillside Mills, 1915; Dunson Hospital, 1916; Mansour's Store, 1917; LaGrange Employment Bureau, 1918

## ORGANIZATIONS

LaGrange Settlement (for Charitable Work Expansion), 1913; Mountville Community Club, 1919; Baxter L. Schaub American Legion Post, 1919; Kiwanis Club (second one in Georgia), 1919; first Boy Scout troop, 1919; first Girl Scout troop, 1919

# HAPPENINGS

Regular letters in the *Reporter* from former publisher, Mrs. Pope Callaway, on her trip around the world, 1910; Harriet Hawkes Memorial Hall dedication at LaGrange Female College, 1911; new post office completed, 1913; Daisy Davies named LaGrange Female College president (only officially named female president in the college's history), 1913; new LaGrange High School building, 1915; earthquake shook county, 1916; North Georgia Conference of Methodist Church met in LaGrange, 1917; Southern Female College closed, 1917; influenza epidemic with many local deaths, 1918; West Point flood, 1919

LaGrange buildings, card postmarked 1914. Those pictured include Unity Cotton Mill, First Methodist Church and Parsonage, Slack Sanitarium, LaGrange High School, Troup County Courthouse and the Confederate Monument.

# 1910s DECADE REVIEW—NATIONALLY

Founding of Boy Scouts of America, 1910; first Father's Day observed in Spokane, Washington, 1910; Girl Scouts founded in Savannah, Georgia, 1912; Congress passed Sixteenth Amendment (income tax), 1913; General

Electric made first electric stoves, irons and toasters, 1913; World War began, 1914; Frigidaire sold first electric refrigerators, 1915; U.S. Coast Guard established, 1915; National Park Service founded, 1916; United States declared war on Germany, 1917; inauguration of Selective Service, 1917; Germany surrendered, ending World War, 1918; influenza epidemic worldwide, 1918; strikes, labor riots in United States, 1919

## Winsome Murmurs from the 1910s

*Congress will probably adjourn about the first of August, provided it doesn't "blow up and bust" before that time.*

*The Alabama Supreme Court has ruled that it is illegal to loan a friend who is sick a glass of liquor.*

*Lost—A $5 dollar bill somewhere near the A.B. and A. Depot in LaGrange Sunday afternoon. Liberal reward will be paid for its return to M.O. Parish, Rte. 3, Mountville.*

*No man impresses us with his importance by simply screwing on a long face and assuming a dignified manner. Owls, also, have somehow acquired the habit of looking wise.*

*After all, it takes the cranks to turn the world.*

*It looks kinder funny to see a fellow with a one-cylinder brain driving a six-cylinder automobile with 15 cents in his pocket.*

*The height of a girl's ambitions is about five feet six, says the Journal; and a bank account that runs into five or six figures.*

*The hobble skirt has not put in its appearance in LaGrange yet, but we are expecting to see it any day.*

*In 1917 we have wheatless days and meatless days and lightless nights; we are also experiencing a boozeless Christmas.*

CHAPTER 4

# The 1920s

From *LaGrange Graphic* and *LaGrange Graphic-Shuttle*

L aGrange grew overnight between New Year's Eve and New Year's Day, January 1, 1920, as the first January issue of the *LaGrange Graphic* reported:

> *LaGrange Grows to Greater Proportions—Last night, December 31, 1919, at midnight, LaGrange burst the bonds of her swaddling clothes and became a city of considerable magnitude. A bill for the charter of Southwest LaGrange was amended so that the corporate limits of the city of LaGrange could be extended two miles from the courthouse in every direction, at midnight, December 31, 1919. This has added a vast area of manufacturing and residential property to the city and it is expected that the population will be increased to such an extent that the number will be close to 25,000.*

This addition included the area of LaGrange around the Callaway and Dunson Mills. This extension increased the population of the newly established public schools in LaGrange, because some of the children of school age living in the newly added area had usually attended schools provided by these mills.

This news was soon followed later in the year by a news report stating, "From the 167th in size of population, LaGrange shows almost as great growth as any city in a list of the cities in the South that have shown great growth. LaGrange went from 167th in 1910, to 64th in size according to

Main Street scene dating from the 1920s, looking north toward the square in downtown LaGrange. *Curt Teich Postcards.*

recent census figures." The *Graphic* story concluded, "Just keep your eyes on LaGrange and watch her continue to grow."

In 1925, according to the report of the Census Bureau calculations, "In population, LaGrange is the sixth largest city in Georgia, after Atlanta, Savannah, Macon, Augusta and Columbus." At that time LaGrange's population was reported at 23,523.

LaGrange remembered its World War heroes, as the newspaper reported, in February 1920, when a detachment of regular army troops from the Fifth Division stationed at Camp Gordon pitched camp on the fairgrounds and gave LaGrange residents an opportunity to see army life in their own town.

Army troops had remained in LaGrange for a week, giving the citizens the opportunity to see some of the most impressive ceremonies of the army—"a formal guard mount on the Courthouse Square, followed by a band concert. A parade followed with several local groups marching with the battle heroes of the late war, all of whom had seen overseas service. A group from Camp Benning joined them for the firing of infantry weapons."

The troops had participated in the planting of memorial trees in town to honor the men from LaGrange who lost their lives in the World War. The service, sponsored by the local chapter of the United Daughters of the Confederacy, was held on February 12. According to the *Graphic*'s report, "A tree was planted for each of the following young men: Jesse Atkinson, Joel Bohannon, McKinley Brock, John Cannon, Hoke Frazier, Ferrell Hamer, Charlie Parker, Amos Payne, Juel Reid, Baxter Schaub, Luther Story, Juel Taylor, Thomas Thomaston and Knox Thompson."

A severe storm swept through West Point and suburban LaGrange on Sunday evening, March 28, 1920. The *Graphic* reported:

> *The LaGrange spirit was manifested everywhere when a storm left death, desolation and destruction in its path on Sunday evening. Twenty-five people were killed and over 100 were injured. Estimated property loss exceeds $1,000,000. Our sorrow is not for the material loss, but over the sadness brought into the homes of our citizens, both white and colored. Our captains of industry will rebuild in the sections laid waste, new and larger plants will be erected, new homes will rear their heads from the wreckage, and that which now lies in ruins, will again become the scene of activity.*

One example of heroism reported after the storm is worthy of special comment. A young Negro girl, Charley Brewer, who was an office girl for Dr. H.W. Terrell, went to the scene of the worst devastation, found Dr. Terrell and worked with him in a temporary hospital he had set up at the courthouse all one night and the following day. The newspaper report stated, "She was one of many local people who demonstrated the spirit of sacrificing personal comforts to help suffering humanity."

Our neighbors in Hogansville were experiencing good times early in this decade. In "Hogansville Happenings," a regular feature of the *Graphic*, the writer of the column reported:

> *Everything and everybody in this good town seem to be wearing the contented smile of prosperity these days. Business is good, health is above average, social activities on every hand, church life flourishing and the outlook for the future is confident. Work on our $70,000 school building is progressing very rapidly, with sixteen recitation rooms and an auditorium that will seat 500 persons.*

A Hogansville Board of Trade was formed in 1920, and New England Southern opened the Stark Mill there. But Hogansville, with all of its progress, had quiet streets at times, as reported in a later column: "Hogansville is not rushed with business just now. In the last three or four days one may look up the street almost any time now and see from one to three or four games of checkers in progress."

In January 1921, the national scene seemed to be often on the mind of the *Graphic*'s editor, as reflected in this series of editorial commentary on problems facing the nation:

> *Our national debt is now more than 25 billions of dollars. Annual interest charges are about one and a quarter billion, all of which we must pay before we can have anything that we can earn for ourselves. We have 250 billions of dollars of property in this country. A ten percent tax would pay the debt and stop the interest at once. Those who have made profits on account of the war should be taxed to pay the debt, and the imposition of such a tax would work no hardship on anyone.*

Two other problems the editor addressed in 1921 remind us that history often repeats itself. He wrote this about unemployment at that time: "More than one million workers in the United States are out of work, which means there are from three million to five million people who are suffering for the necessities of life."

There was also a drug problem in the United States then, and he wrote that "there is a great army of men and women marching toward certain physical and moral destruction. They have given up allegiance to our country and home and society. They are drug addicts."

He reported that during a ten-month period, records showed, "564,000 pounds of opium have been brought into the United States, representing nearly thirty grains for every man, woman and child in this country." The editor continued: "Our great country is consuming ten times as much opium as any other country, according to Dr. Royal S. Copeland. If this is true, and we have no right to dispute it, this nation is fast drifting to destruction, because a nation is no stronger than its individual citizens."

If these examples were not enough to make us see that "there is nothing new under the sun," read the editor's opinion on another problem facing the nation at that time. This "prophet of old" wrote: "There has never been such a wave of crime, from petty larceny to murder, as is passing over this country at this time. Crimes are being committed in high places and in low places; by men and women of high rank and low rank; for small offenses, large offenses and for no offense. Indeed, it seems as if we are living in the last days, if the prophecy of the Scriptures is true."

In November 1921, Mayor S.H. Dunson of LaGrange issued a proclamation designating Armistice Day a holiday in the city of LaGrange and "directing that it shall be so observed by all city employees." He also requested all the store owners and other business employers to allow their employees a day to observe appropriately the spirit of the day.

The *Graphic*'s coverage of this news also included a request that "because 11 o'clock in the morning had been selected as the exact time of the signing of the Armistice, the Mayor asks that every citizen and inhabitant of LaGrange observe two minutes immediately following 11 o'clock in silent devotion. All manufacturing enterprises of the city and vicinity are asked to sound their whistles beginning at 10:57 and continuing until the hour of 11 o'clock."

The following year, in 1922, the *Graphic*'s editor made the following suggestion in an editorial:

> *On one corner of our Court Square stands a monument erected to the memory of Confederate soldiers. The heart of everyone, who cherishes the uniform of Gray as a hallmark of nobility, beats with a just pride when he looks upon that silent sentinel guarding the dawn and sunset over our happy town. But on the other corner of our Court Square stands idle, blank space, erected by the negligent hands of Forgetfulness to commemorate the deeds of the sons of Troup County who gave their lives in the recent World War. American Patriots, Attention! We must erect on the Court Square a block of granite, capped with a "Doughboy" sentinel. Post that sentinel there to tell the unborn generations that in yonder cemetery in Flanders Fields sleep American heroes—peacefully awaiting the reveille of the eternal morning to rouse them from a soldier's rest.*

In August 1923, the Baxter L. Schaub Post of the American Legion of Honor, organized in LaGrange after the war and named for the first LaGrange boy to die during the World War, adopted the idea of erecting a memorial statue on the public square in honor of "Troup County sons who were called to the colors and saw service in the World War." At that time they were asking residents of the city and county to contribute five dollars each to finance the memorial, according to a report in the *Graphic*. This project was never completed.

The women of LaGrange, who were members of the LaGrange Woman's Club, began their own plans for a memorial for the soldiers of the World War at the end of the previous decade. Their memorial was to be in the

LaGrange Memorial Library, memorial to World War I servicemen, was built in 1925 as a project of the Woman's Club. The new building was on a different site in 1975.

form of a library, meant to be "the nucleus for a greater library in the future, as necessary funds are available."

With the determination and efforts of members of the Woman's Club, and additional funds raised by the Rotary Club of LaGrange, this dream became a full reality in 1926, with the erection of a handsome building to house the memorial library's books.

In October of that year, the *Graphic* printed this notice:

> *Library Dedication on Armistice Day—Mrs. Clifford Smith, president of the LaGrange Woman's Club, announces that the exercises dedicating the new library building to the Troup County World War veterans will be held on Armistice Day, November 11. The dedication exercises will be one of the main features in the celebration of Armistice Day in LaGrange this year.*

For many years the Woman's Club provided the salary of the librarian and had a meeting room for the club meetings and events in the building with the library. When the library became a public facility in the 1970s, the books were moved into a new building, and the old building became a governmental office.

In this decade, readers of the *Graphic* enjoyed the humor of the editor reflected in his thoughts on the automobile, as well as in his thoughts on more serious subjects. This is an example:

> *The invasion of the automobiles in this country far surpasses the Bolshevist in financial havoc. More money is invested in these things than in all the banks in Georgia, and the money goes where the "woodbine twineth." A friend of mine, who has had experience with one or two cars, tells me no man should own one, unless he has an income of at least $12,000 a year.*

A $100,000 grant to pave Troup County roads was welcome news about that time. It hit the front page of the *Graphic* with this headline: "One Hundred Thousand Dollars for Paved Roads."

The news report, from a reliable authority, said that Troup County was to get from the National Highway Department $100,000 to be used to pave ten miles of roads throughout the county. It was understood that the roads leading to Hogansville and West Point were to be paved five miles each way from LaGrange. The story added, "This doubtless will be the beginning of permanent roads in Troup County. It is hoped so, at least."

In the same issue of the newspaper, it was reported that the work of grading had begun on Main Street in LaGrange, preparatory to paving the street. The writer added, "With the other paving already completed and proposed, LaGrange is expected to have more paved streets than possibly any city of its size in the state."

Callaway Mills was organized into one company in 1922. This was business news of great interest in LaGrange. The *Graphic* reported that the Unity Cotton Mills, Elm City Cotton Mills of LaGrange, Milstead Manufacturing Company of Milstead and Manchester Cotton Mills of Manchester were organizing their own selling agency, Callaway Mills Inc. The officers reported were "Fuller E. Callaway, chairman of the board; Cason J. Callaway, president; Ely R. Callaway, vice-president and treasurer; and W.A. Drisler, secretary."

A five-month drought hit Troup County in 1925, and that year became known as "the year people could walk across the Chattahoochee River," according to the *Graphic*. LaGrange suffered along with the entire county.

By August of that year, LaGrange was face to face with one of the most serious water shortages in its history, according to Mayor G.C. Hunter, who

City Park, La Grange, Ga.—2

McLendon's Pond was once in a recreation park. It was used for early First Baptist Church baptisms. No pond remains, and Springdale Drive homes are now built on the site.

was quoted in the *Graphic* saying, "The water system is being turned on for only one hour during the day in order that the supply being held for an emergency will not be consumed."

The newspaper reported that the Swift Company had offered the city the use of its well and the water wagon was bringing in a supply of water to the public square to provide drinking water on a regular basis. It was announced, "M.F. McLendon has given the city the use of his well at McLendon's Park for at least twelve months and arrangements are being made to install a pump there as early as possible to obtain that supply."

By October 1925, the city waterworks was again in operation, the newspaper reported, after "passing through one of the most trying and hazardous periods in its history." The editor warned, "The water system must be extended, or LaGrange and her people are going to suffer irreparable loss in growth and development."

All during this decade, federal authorities were working out standard traffic laws and regulations in an effort to reduce automobile accidents. Numerous reports were published in the *Graphic* to keep local citizens informed of developments. One editorial addressed speed limits as follows:

*The national conference on street and highway safety, in session in Atlantic City recently, decided upon the following speed limits which every section of the country will be asked to adopt: 35 miles an hour in the open country; 20 miles an hour in residential districts; 15 miles an hour in business districts; 10 miles an hour passing schools and crossing railroad intersections; four miles an hour crossing sidewalks to or from alleys or private driveways.*

A front-page story in the *Graphic* in April 1926 brought a news item that became of greater importance to this part of Georgia through the next few decades. A headline announced that Franklin D. Roosevelt, a former assistant secretary of the navy, had bought the well-known resort at Warm Springs from George Foster Peabody, also from the state of New York, the principal owner of the corporation that owned the resort at that time. The purchase price was not given, but a good description of the property was. It read, "The property consists of several thousands of acres of land, a hotel, several cottages and swimming pools, together with the springs which are said to flow at the rate of 1,800 gallons per minute. Mr. Roosevelt expects to make the property an all-the-year-round resort. Separate pools will be provided for invalids, according to Mr. Roosevelt."

In September 1927, the *Graphic* reported, "The latest gathering place in LaGrange, the very newest thing to do, is to meet your friends under the scuppernong arbor at the country club. The abundance of fruit has supplied the entire club membership for two weeks now with no sign of giving out."

This would have been referring to the Highland Country Club, which was formed in 1923.

At Thanksgiving that same year, the newspaper reported that the turkeys in LaGrange were "getting fatter every hour as they were being prepared for slaughter the next Thursday."

Mrs. R.T. Segrest, who lived on Vernon Street, was among those in the city who had bought turkeys early to avoid the last-minute rush and "the bum birds," according to the *Graphic*. The report went on, as follows:

*The morning after she bought the bird, a servant went to feed him and he wasn't there. A day elapsed, and neither the turkey came home, nor did any kidnappers offer to return the bird for ransom. The next day somebody, in looking about the back yard, happened to look into a barrel. There was the turkey. This turkey probably figured that as Thanksgiving and his doom grew near, it was up to him to make himself scarce in the best way possible. He did, but unsuccessfully.*

The 1920s decade closed locally in 1929 with the dedication of the Callaway Memorial Tower, built with funds given for this purpose by employees of the Callaway Mills and others, following the death of Mr. Fuller E. Callaway in 1928. His millworkers, as well as the entire area, grieved at the loss of this wonderful man. Mr. Callaway's death and the dedication of the tower were reported in depth in the *LaGrange Graphic* and in the *Shuttle*. Coverage of the dedication of the tower appeared in the *LaGrange News* and *Graphic-Shuttle* after the newspapers merged in June 1929.

Callaway Tower, 1929, a memorial tribute to philanthropist Fuller E. Callaway, who died in 1928. The tower was funded by mill employees and other friends.

It seems appropriate to acknowledge here that the citizens of LaGrange, and beyond, have been blessed through the years by the philanthropy of Mr. and Mrs. Callaway and their children and grandchildren, through grants made by the foundations established and maintained by them. Their financial support has added greatly to the quality of life of this entire area, by the generous gifts for religious, educational, medical and cultural construction and advantages they have provided. This benevolence continues today, made possible by descendants in the Hudson and Callaway families.

The LaGrange newspapers reported the stock market crash in 1929, the year that marked the beginning of the Great Depression nationally, and the devastating effects it would have on the local economy of LaGrange, continuing into the next decade.

# MOSAIC MUSINGS FROM THE 1920s

*It is reported daily that people are "going crazy" and are being sent to the asylum on account of the "Ouija Board." Verily a great many people are giving heed to seducing spirits, and doctrines of devils.*

*Man alive: When our women folks go into the jury boxes, there'll be much commotion in the court house. Young men will see visions and old men will dream dreams. And as for Sullivan, Lovvorn and Martin, why Solomon, in all his glory, was not arrayed like these promising attorneys will be on that glad day.*

*Another thing! When women practice law, if the jury be composed of men only, and a smart young woman appears on one side, woe to the squires on the other side. Even great lawyers like Lovejoy, Mooty, Wyatt, Thompson, Moon et al would stand about as much chance gaining their case, as a bobtail calf in fly time. Yes sir, I'd prefer a flapper to either one, and this is not discounting their ability.*

*About the only difference between the flapper and "flappee," insofar as their heads appear, is in the attitude of bobbed hair. The flapper bobs half way the neck, while the "flappee" cuts near the top of the head.*

*I advise young men of this progressive era to at once become "knickers" if they expect to harmonize with the flappers. Old men will rather look askance at the new order of dress, and take it slowly; and tall sycamore youngsters, a few of whom are hereabouts, may look rather grotesque about the shanks in knickerbockers, but will go along with the gang with padded calves. It's coming!*

*Today you know everybody rides in automobiles, or flies, plays golf, shoots crap, plays the piano with their feet, goes to the movies nightly, smokes cigarettes, drinks Ruckus Juice, blames the H.C. of L. (high cost of living) on the Republicans; they never go to bed the same day they get up, and they think they are having a wonderful time. These are days of "suffragetting," profiteering, excess taxes, and prohibition, and if you think life is worth living, I wish you a Happy New Year.*

*Since 1776 we have drifted far from the fundamental principles upon which this nation was founded. If the Democrats will trot out Henry Ford in the next presidential race, he will sweep the country like an avalanche. Mr. Ford has horse and mule sense combined, and the people believe in his justice, fairness and sound Americanism. It's a little early, but I put him in nomination now.*

*The big John Brown Tabernacle in LaGrange was inadequate to seat the throngs who came to hear Sousa in concert Monday night. Hotels and all available rooms were filled for the night by the great band members and visitors who were here to hear the program. Many of the city's neighbors joined her in a mighty ovation to the greatest living entertainer and the world's best band. The perfect naturalness, the simplicity of manner, the modesty, the utter lack of ostentation on the part of the great bandmaster were beautiful to see. The crowd thrilled and marched and danced and sang national airs, and even jazzed and laughed with Sousa. To the sponsoring Rotarians, congratulations.*

*When you see a fellow coming down the road with a pistol in each pocket, two or three sticking from his boot tops, a couple of automatic shot guns swung across his shoulders, you immediately conclude that he is either a fool or looking for a fight, and dangerous in either case. That's just exactly the way the nations of the world today go strutting around before each other. The same conclusion fits the latter case just as logically as the first one.*

## OPENINGS/FOUNDINGS

LaGrange Chamber of Commerce, 1920; Charlie Joseph's fruit stand/sandwiches on Main Street, 1920; public library, 1921; LaGrange Elks Club, 1922; Highland Country Club, 1923; East Depot School for Negro Children, 1923; Southwest LaGrange Y Pool, 1923; LaGrange Welfare Association, 1924; LaGrange Memorial Library, dedicated to memory of men who died in World War, LaGrange Woman's Club project, 1926; LaGrange City Hall, 1927; Humane Society, 1927

## ORGANIZATIONS/CHURCHES

Church of Christ in LaGrange (a continuation of Disciples of Christ founded in West Point in 1853), 1920; LaGrange Chapter of the Daughters of the American Revolution chartered, 1920; Southwest LaGrange Baptist Church and Southwest LaGrange Methodist Church, 1920; LaGrange Rotary Club chartered, 1923; Loyal Order of Moose, 1927; LaGrange Cotillion Club, 1927; Lions Club, 1929

## HAPPENINGS

Annexation of property in the city extended two miles in every direction from courthouse, 1920; LaGrange High School won state football championship, 1924; Golden Age of Radio brought radio parties to local and county homes, 1925; Charleston dance craze reached LaGrange, 1925; John Philip Sousa's band concert in LaGrange sponsored by Rotary Club, 1926; Camp Viola's first summer camp for children, 1927; Narcotic Education Week observed in LaGrange, 1928; dedication of Callaway Memorial Tower, 1929; dedication of First Presbyterian Church's new building, 1929

## 1920s DECADE REVIEW—NATIONALLY

Nineteenth Amendment ratified, giving women right to vote, 1920; Prohibition law passed, 1920; Veterans Bureau established, 1921; national juvenile crime wave, 1922; thirteen telephones to every one hundred people, 1923; first motion picture with sound shown in New York, 1923;

Scopes Trial in Tennessee—upheld right of the state to ban teaching of evolution in public schools, 1925; beginning of Golden Age of Radio, 1925; establishment of Army Air Corps, 1926; Lindbergh's first solo flight across Atlantic Ocean, 1927; penicillin discovered, first antibiotic, 1928; U.S. stock market crashed, beginning the Great Depression, 1929; passenger air service began in Atlanta, 1929

## WINSOME MURMURS FROM THE 1920S

*The average street dress of today looks about like a bathing suit did 15 years ago. What will a bathing suit of 15 years hence look like?*

*Despite politics, court week, the boll weevil, or any other thing of only passing interest, the courthouse checkers game goes on, uninterrupted, undisturbed.*

*A woman's contest is brewing—the bow legs are clamorous for long skirts on the grounds they haven't a fair show, while the short skirts say, "let well enough alone."*

*A local merchant recently made the statement, and it was vouched for by other merchants present, that there is more money spent in LaGrange for ladies' silk hose than for men's clothing. Had you thought that maybe, after all, hosiery manufacturers are responsible for the short skirt?*

*This drifted in from the high school. "How is a girl with bobbed hair like a bungalow?" She has a painted front, a shingled top and an empty attic.*

*Probably the remotest control of all remote controls nowadays is parental control.*

*There is going to be a shaking of the dry bones in LaGrange some of these days, and when it happens there is going to be a great awakening. Get busy!*

*London doctors say that if the women persist in having their hair cut "A la Male" that they are sure to become bald-headed just like men.*

*It is well to pray for deliverance from evil, but don't overlook the fact that a gun loaded with buckshot is a fine safeguard against night riders and burglars.*

*There has been enough preaching in LaGrange during the last two months to save the world, if salvation depends on preaching.*

 *Dear old Congress, having resurrected itself, will now proceed to do a little something and a lot of nothing.*

*One person out of every twelve is now on our government pay roll and the other eleven have ambitions.*

*When you stop to think about that dollar you laid away for a rainy day; if you still have it, compared with what it was fifteen years ago, it is worth just about thirty cents.*

*A newspaper man has found the happiest man in the world and he lives in North Georgia. "He has six fiddles, ten children, thirteen hounds, a deaf and dumb wife and a moonshine still that has never been spotted by the government."*

## CHAPTER 5

# The 1930s

From *LaGrange Daily News*

With the beginning of the 1930s, LaGrange residents found themselves in a changing world. The Depression, which had started in 1929, continued to affect the lives of many local and area citizens—especially the farmers, millworkers, teachers and many city employees who were faced with layoffs, shorter hours of work and delayed salaries. Some local bankers and businessmen also had to change their lifestyles drastically, according to reports in the *Daily News*.

In October 1930, the *Daily News* reported in its news story, "Stock Market in Violent Break," that the stock market had "plunged downward on October 9, after a break in steel and the announcement of the failure of Prince & Whitely, one of the largest commission bonus houses in the nation's financial district."

New lows of the year had rolled out on the Wall Street ticker, bringing with them the resulting loss of millions of dollars in paper value after the commission house failure had been announced.

In November of that same year, in the "On the Square" column in the *Daily News*, readers were told what one barber in town was experiencing:

> *What's the first thing people cut down on when times begin to get hard?*
> *According to John Hill, at Williams and Hill Barber Shop in LaGrange,*
> *it is shaves, then hair cuts. "They think they can save money by shaving*
> *themselves," he said. "Then they go longer without getting a haircut. Then,*
> *when they do come in, they figure they're getting their money's worth."*

In December 1931, LaGrange teachers were receiving checks for back pay, as reported in the *News*: "The city of LaGrange played Santa Claus today to 95 local school teachers and sent them checks for half-a-month's salary due since August. Funds to cover the checks were obtained from tax payments beginning to come in before the books close on December 20."

Many city employees had to take salary cuts in 1932, and city officials' "stipends" were also cut. In April, teachers in the city system were told that their salaries would be cut by 10 percent for the next school year. At this same time, Troup County teachers and bus drivers were receiving their March salary checks because the county Board of Education had received state funds making this possible, according to continuing reports in the *Daily News*.

The young debutantes in LaGrange were so concerned about the economy that they did something about it, as readers of the *News* were told in 1932. Members of the LaGrange Cotillion Club reported that "71 people had joined their local 'Penny Club.'" Club members had placed 106 jars around town from which they collected pennies, contributed by LaGrange friends for a fund to provide work for the unemployed in the community. There were 71 members of the "Penny a Meal Club" in LaGrange, and the jars for collection of the pennies were placed regularly in thirty-five locations around town. In December 1932, more than six thousand pennies were collected from the members and other donors.

The newspaper reported that Captain H.V. Lovick of the Salvation Army supervised the unemployed men who needed temporary work, and Miss Viola Burks, the head of the local Welfare Association, saw that many needy women were paid a small compensation for work they did, such as sewing, quilting and laundering.

Later in the 1930s, following the election of President Franklin D. Roosevelt, the introduction of his New Deal programs put many unemployed people back to work in jobs that also strengthened the local infrastructure.

The 1930s decade brought a new excitement and meaningful celebration "On the Hill," the name the local college has always been called because of its natural elevation.

In 1931, the college celebrated its 100th anniversary all year, with special observances at graduation in the spring and special events planned for the fall, as students returned for the new college year. A former Georgia governor, John M. Slaton, was the graduation speaker, according to the *Daily News*.

LaGrange City Swimming Pool, a 1935 project of the Works Progress Administration. It was remodeled in 1991. *Silvercraft-Dexter Press.*

The newspaper published a special college centennial edition on October 8, 1931, to commemorate the institution's special anniversary. The edition contained many wonderful old photographs and a collection of nostalgic memories of the college's colorful past. An especially appropriate editorial written for that occasion follows:

> *LaGrange Claims Many Citizens Due to Successful College Romances— Always the girls "On the Hill" have been more than attractive to the young men of the city. From the '31s of the 19th century to the '31s of the 20th century, one of the main problems of the college faculty has been to hide the young ladies from the young men—not that the young men are not desirable, but the young ladies are in school and have work to do. Work and beaux don't mix except occasionally. Despite the precautions that may have been taken to keep the young ladies' minds on school books, a number of college-city romances have developed that have resulted in LaGrange winning a number of charming young matrons as permanent residents. These recruits from Dan Cupid have not only been students, but some faculty members, who have seen fit to leave the school room and come down into the city and assume domestic duties.*

During this decade, in 1934, the 103-year-old institution changed its name from LaGrange Female College to LaGrange College in a new charter, perhaps as an omen of events to come.

College alumnae, as well as all patrons of the historic institution, felt a special pride when their well-loved old school was mentioned in Margaret Mitchell's popular novel, *Gone with the Wind*, released in 1936. Scarlett O'Hara's beloved "Aunt Pittypat" was said to have attended the "LaGrange Female Institute," an earlier name for the school. The *Daily News* reported this recognition as "a timely tribute to the local college."

A front-page story in the newspaper in the early 1930s, releasing statistics from Bureau of the Census bulletins, showed a marked decline in illiteracy in Troup County, information that was received with pleasure by LaGrange and Troup County educators. The 1930 census revealed that "the total percentage of illiteracy in Troup County is 8.4 percent, compared with 18.3 percent in 1920. Total Troup County population is reported to be 36,097."

The illiteracy reduction could have been helped by a project of the LaGrange public schools, as described in this item from the *Daily News* in February 1930:

> *300 Adults Now Studying How to Read, Write—The probability of continuing the night classes of the city which have been successfully conducted for the last four weeks, was discussed at a meeting held yesterday. Classes are being held at Harwell Avenue School, Dawson Street, Dunson, Unity, Hill Street, Southwest LaGrange and the different colored schools."*

At that meeting, the newspaper reported that F.F. Rowe, superintendent of the LaGrange public schools, had announced that there were more than three hundred pupils enrolled in night classes. These adult education classes were expected to continue for another month. At the end of the course, a diploma was given to each person who could read simple English and write his or her own name legibly. Many persons of foreign birth took advantage of the location of Harwell Avenue School to attend the classes there.

The LaGrange Opportunity School, another project of the LaGrange school system, was also in the news, as the newspaper reported later in 1930. H.W. Caldwell, director of the Opportunity School and one of the state's outstanding vocational education workers, was invited to address the United States Senate Committee on Vocational Education in Washington, D.C., as Georgia's representative. His address was based on the work that was being done in LaGrange, and in Georgia, in the matter of vocational training schools. The *Daily News* report added: "State vocational board officials consider the LaGrange Opportunity School to be one of the most efficient units in Georgia. It is operated under the city of LaGrange school system and Mr. Caldwell is the chairman of the vocational committee of the board."

An interesting bit of trivia about the local schools not found in the local newspaper was found in a masterfully researched and written history, *The LaGrange Public Schools*, by Dr. Nancy Lillian Clark and William Wates Keller, both deceased. It offers an unusual glimpse into the schools in the '30s: "For several years in the '30s, teachers were issued notices that only single lady teachers would be employed. Married women, already in the system, would continue, but if a lady teacher decided to marry, she should resign."

In May 1930, a headline and story in the *Daily News* announced that local citizens were applauding the report that "LaGrange has become a full-fledged zoned city following passage of a new zoning ordinance by the mayor and city council."

This was welcome news for a growing city. The following front-page news item that came shortly thereafter prompted local interest to take off, understandably, in another popular direction:

> *Airways Operation officers from Maxwell Field in Montgomery expect to complete a survey of Callaway Field with government aviators within a few days. The survey is being conducted only for the purpose of determining whether the field can be used as an intermediate stop between Atlanta and Montgomery. After being told the airport road lies outside the city limits of LaGrange, Lt. Philip Rolls suggested that Troup County should do the work on the road and allow the city to share in the cost of the work. He said a good access road would be necessary if such a project were to be undertaken.*

Later, a notice was published in the *Daily News* that Troup County was planning to work on the airport road because the road was impassable after heavy rains.

Interest in the airport and air travel, in general, continued all during the early '30s, and the *Daily News* carried frequent items of interest to its air-minded readers. An item on the possibility of airplanes affecting the architecture of the future follows:

> *When we try to peer into the future, we take it for granted that the American city of 2030 A.D. will have more skyscrapers than we have today. Francis Keally, an architect, writing in an architectural publication, doesn't think so. He believes skyscrapers will almost disappear during the new century and*

*there will be flat-topped buildings of a uniform height. Why? Because of the airplane. Skyscrapers will be a traffic hazard, so they will be replaced by low, wide buildings whose roofs will be landing fields.*

A truly prophetic editorial in November 1931 reported:

*An airplane flew through the low-hanging clouds and mists and landed at the local airport yesterday. The tourists of the sky were from Maine en route to New Orleans. They landed here to await more favorable weather conditions. Visitors who drop in suddenly from the sky will ever arouse interest and curiosity. The time is not too distant when the air will be filled with caravans of commerce and airplanes will be as commonplace as automobiles are now. Yet people will never become entirely casual about the accomplishments of man's conquering gravity.*

In December 1933, a long-awaited official announcement about the airport was reported in the *Daily News*. The Georgia PWA Commission had approved the building of a new airport at LaGrange. The report said, "The project represents an expenditure of $76,731, and will employ 580 men for a period of about eight weeks. When completed, it will be one of the best in the state, being slightly larger than Candler Field near Atlanta. Location of the new field will be precisely on the ground known formerly as Callaway Field. This field has been taken over by the city of LaGrange."

The local airport never met all the expectations of the writer of that report, but it has always offered great assistance to local efforts to bring new industries to LaGrange and to the county.

In an effort to bring this commentary on the airport to a close for this decade, it seems appropriate to quote from *Treasures of Troup County*, a pictorial and excellently researched history of Troup County written by Glenda Major and Clark Johnson, well known for their love for local history and their journalistic abilities as authors. Clark Johnson is Troup County historian. Their book offered this further reference to the LaGrange airfield: "Troup County has had an airfield since the 1910s. In 1936, the Works Progress Administration built the Callaway Airport. The site was expanded during World War II when the Civil Aeronautics Administration added three 5000 foot runways. When the war ended in 1945, the military turned the airport back over to the city of LaGrange."

There will be more about the further development of the LaGrange-Callaway Airport in future decades.

# Musings from America's Greatest Little City

Through the years, accomplished LaGrange citizens in various walks of life have provided leadership to state and national organizations and institutions.

In this decade, in the year 1931, the *Daily News* brought this fact to its readers in an intelligible way in an item entitled "A LaGrange Man Is," followed by a list of local men with such leadership positions, or accomplishments they had made, at that time. This included the following:

> *Cason J. Callaway, president, American Cotton Manufacturers Association; Hatton J. Lovejoy, president, Georgia Bar Association; Robert T. Williams, chairman, executive board, Georgia Elks Association; H.C. Woodruff, president, Fourth District Convention of County Commissioners of Georgia; Ely R. Callaway, lay leader, Georgia Baptist Convention; Frank R. Jenkins, president, Southern Union College, Wadley, Alabama; Ulrich R. Phillips, author, prize-winning volume, "Life and Letters in the Old South" and Searcy B. Slack, bridge engineer, Georgia Highway Board.*

In a May 1933 edition of the *Daily News*, there was an intriguing story on the retirement of an old jail register that contained the "colorful records of the county jail for the past quarter century." Some of it is reprinted here:

> *The old county jail register has been filled. This interesting old tome is a cross-section of life itself, the sordid side, but it is life nevertheless. The last name was entered in this big old book yesterday, and the pages of a new register were opened. A total of 8,184 people have been committed to the Troup County jail in 22 years. The varied list of crimes ranges from wife-whipping (a misdemeanor in those good old days), to murder in the first degree. Crimes directly linked to liquor are in the preponderance. Many entries were for "selling booze." Some other offenses were cow stealing, throwing rocks at a church, stealing a buggy, taking a drink on the highway and leaving home. An inquiry as to the nature of that last offense disclosed that it was for abandoning minor children. The old book will be filed in the archives of county records. Students of criminology and social problems could find it a source of valuable information.*

Clouds of unrest were gathering over Europe in September 1933, when the front page of the *Daily News* carried the following item:

> *Horrible Deeds Laid to Nazis—Horrifying facts relating to the persecution of Jews, intellectuals and communists in Germany under the new Nazi*

*regime are related in "The Brown Book of the Hitler Terror," prepared by the "World Committee for the Victims of German Fascism" and published this week in the United States. The book includes an appendix containing a list of 250 "murders" for which the committee says it holds authentic documents of proof.*

Rumblings from the Pacific side of the world were reported that same year in December in the *Daily News*. "Military and naval officers of the United States were amazed," the newspaper reported, "by the accurate descriptions of American cruisers and warships contained in pamphlets found in a confiscated shipment of magazines, printed in Japan and held by custom authorities in Honolulu. Profusely illustrated fiction described an imaginative American-Japanese War in 1936 and the Japanese capture of Hawaii." The newspaper report concluded with the statement, "Army authorities have begun an immediate investigation into this matter."

By February 1934, the ensuing "investigation" apparently brought this response from the Japanese, and LaGrange citizens read this item in the *Daily News*:

*Japan does not want and does not intend to go to war with anybody. Leaders of the Japanese army, navy and the government are unanimous. Americans who consider themselves observers in Tokyo energetically agree with their declarations. They say all "anti-American statements in the press," common a year ago, have entirely disappeared since Foreign Minister Koki Hirota took office. They somewhat credit the declaration of friendship to the popularity of United States Ambassador to Japan Joseph Grew.*

This statement from Japan brought some reassurance about our diplomatic efforts there, but fears of problems with Germany seemed to escalate in August 1934, when LaGrange residents read in the *Daily News* that Adolf Hitler had taken sole command of the German government on August 21. At the moment that President Paul von Hindenburg died, Hitler became president-chancellor. The newspaper reported that the merger of the two offices was "legalized at a cabinet meeting by a special law possible under the emergency powers of the Nazi dictatorship. Hitler, the 'Fuehrer,' the self-proclaimed 'man of destiny,' is now in the position he picked for himself more than 11 years ago in a Munich beer cellar."

In "Now and Then," a regular front-page column in the *Daily News*, in March 1935, readers found references to the obvious military build-up in Germany. "France and Italy joined Great Britain today [March 21] in protesting against Germany's rearmament, but the Reich stood firm in her position that the other powers already have abrogated the Versailles Treaty. German officials showed no concern, apparently secure in their belief that Germany was within her rights and that pending negotiations would lessen the European armament crisis." The report continued, adding that "the council would meet in April and it was hoped that a vote condemning Germany might be avoided. Condemnation could only bring defiance from Germany."

In April, the "Now and Then" columnist made further comments on the problems in Europe when he wrote:

> *Status of the European situation about Germany's rearmament seems to be that the little nations won't sign their names to a note because the big nations won't change the phrases "damn Hitler" to something soft and apologetic like "blawst the man." And still they say Lloyds of London is offering even money on European war within six months.*

Three months later, in July 1935, the headline "War Looms" sounded far more ominous, and the editor asked his readers, "Do we in LaGrange read our newspapers with a realization that the import of the happenings of the day as recorded may have a profound effect upon our personal destinies and accomplishments?" Then he answered his own question with, "Probably not," adding:

> *How many of us have been reading the accounts of the Italian-Ethiopian controversy with the full realization of what that quarrel may mean to us? Today it seems impossible to think that the United States could be drawn into the controversy between Italy and Ethiopia. Tomorrow it may be inevitable. It will take a united militant sentiment against war to keep our own country out of the conflict, once it becomes widespread in Europe.*

As students and teachers were returning to schools, colleges and universities in September 1935, an interesting article appeared in the *Daily News*. It reminded its readers of the wide influence local teachers and professors have on educational institutions out of town and out of state, as well as here at home.

It was inspiring, and somewhat surprising, to read that "LaGrange's intellectual influence will be felt widely and directly in at least seven states this fall, as teachers ranging from the primary level in elementary schools, to graduate departments of great universities, leave their homes in LaGrange to assume and reassume the responsibilities of one of humanity's sacred trusts."

The story went on, pointing out that "some half-a-hundred young local men and women will serve this year in the legion of pedagogues whose activity makes of young Americans world-citizens of tomorrow."

The seven states represented were Alabama, Florida, North Carolina, South Carolina, Massachusetts and New York, along with other locations in Georgia. Some colleges and universities were included in the educational institutions served. "Many of these teachers and professors were educated at LaGrange College," according to the *Daily News* report.

That same month, an item in the *Daily News* reported a tribute to a well-known and highly respected citizen of the West Point area, LaFayette Lanier Jr., a textile mill official with the West Point Manufacturing Company, who had died five years earlier.

A memorial had been unveiled on September 26 in Langdale, Alabama, in Mr. Lanier's memory. According to the news report, "The memorial, a beautiful marble fountain, is located in a park named in honor of Mr. Lanier, across the highway from a school, also named in his memory."

The story added that "20,000 residents of Georgia and the Valley area made contributions to the memorial fund."

Three important openings, with long-lasting significance, were reported in the *Daily News* in 1936. These were the opening of St. Peter's Church, the first Catholic church in LaGrange; plans for the opening of City-County Hospital on Vernon Road, built to replace the old Dunson Hospital, which

City-County Hospital, opened in 1937 on Vernon Road. It replaced Dunson Hospital and was the forerunner of West Georgia Medical Center, built on the same site in 1974. It has undergone many expansions. *Curt Teich Postcards.*

was no longer adequate for the growing medical needs of the area; and the opening of the Clark-Holder Clinic, founded by two local doctors, Dr. Wallace H. Clark and Dr. James Holder, which brought to LaGrange many new specialty physicians through the years.

An important news story in the *Daily News*, and one that changed the downtown scene permanently, reported a fire that destroyed the Troup County Courthouse on Court Square on November 5, 1936. A part of this report follows: "A fire of unknown origin started in the afternoon. Citizens, using the 'bucket brigade' method, saved almost all of the important county records. In spite of the court's being in session, everyone in the building escaped except the county nurse and one of her patients, who died when they jumped from an upper story window."

At the end of the 1930s decade, in 1939, the *Daily News* reported the opening of the new Troup County Courthouse on Ridley Avenue. This brought a "new look" to downtown LaGrange. For the first time, there was no building in the center of the square, and local citizens were discussing what should be done about the vacant square.

National news in the local daily in 1939 brought this startling headline: "Germany Invades Poland." World War II had begun in Europe.

The second Troup County Courthouse, built in 1904, replaced the 1829 building. This courthouse burned in 1936. The new building is located off the square.

# Mosaic Musings from the 1930s

*An increasingly large number of employers are refusing to accept a girl who has reached the age of 30. Twenty-nine stands as a ripe old age, the last year in which it is possible for a maiden to attempt economic independence. In a recent survey of employment agencies and industries which employ women, it was revealed that those who have already obtained places in the business world may find themselves classified in the ranks of the feeble on reaching their 34th birthdays. It is a generally accepted fact that a woman's chances of marriage are on the decrease after 25. If her business opportunities are to be placed on a sliding scale, it is quite probable that she will brush up on her biscuits and jam instead of her typing. It would seem that it is wiser for a maiden to prepare a batch of applesauce, and leave the bacon for Adam to bring home.*

*It has seemed lately as if a stock market that got drunk three years ago on the champagne of prosperity was capable of getting drunk on ginger ale. It is evident that business is improving, and there is now a good reason to think that business will continue to improve if Wall Street and its amateur gamblers and investors will behave themselves.*

*The new city code, soon to come from the presses, contains corrections by omitting a few amusing regulations. Among them is an ordinance preventing the driving of mules in droves across Court Square. Progress in the machine age has changed many ordinances that were very necessary when written.*

*Separated by a distance of two miles, newspapermen from the metropolitan press were able to speak and see each other yesterday by means of a new two-way telephone-television system developed by the American Telephone & Telegraph Company.*

*Perhaps no city in the country the size of LaGrange can boast of churches which work with more accord and mutual sympathy in the greatest of all businesses than do those here in LaGrange. On the bulletin board of the First Presbyterian Church appears the following message: "Do not fail to hear Dr. Carter Helm Jones at First Baptist Church this week."*

## OPENINGS/FOUNDINGS

LaGrange Theater on Main Street, 1930; Hill Street School, 1931; LaGrange Swimming Pool, 1935; local office of Federal Housing Administration, 1935; Gallant-Belk Store, 1935; St. Peter's Catholic Church, first Catholic church in LaGrange, 1936; Clark-Holder Clinic, 1936; City-County Hospital, 1937; new Troup County Courthouse, 1939; LaGrange Field Office of Social Security Administration, 1939

## ORGANIZATIONS

American Legion Auxiliary, 1931; LaGrange Education Association, 1937; Men's Junior Chamber of Commerce, 1938

## HAPPENINGS

*LaGrange Daily News* now a merger of *LaGrange Reporter*, *LaGrange Graphic-Shuttle*, 1930; LaGrange College celebration of its 100th anniversary, 1931; Callaway Mills consolidated into one corporation, 1932; Clifford L. Smith published *The History of Troup County*, 1933; Cotton Festival with parade and street dance, 1934; Warren Temple Methodist Church Building completed, 1934; fifteen local churches held simultaneous revivals, 1935; countywide drive for child healthcare, 1935; Troup County Courthouse burned, 1936; new Troup County Courthouse completed, 1939

The Troup County Courthouse was completed in 1939 at a new location, Ridley Avenue. This is the third of four courthouses and the first one located off the square. *Curt Teich Postcards.*

# 1930s DECADE REVIEW—NATIONALLY

Veterans Administration established, 1930; favorite cookbook for women, *The Joy of Cooking*, published by Mrs. Irma Rombauer, 1931; "Star-Spangled Banner" named official United States national anthem, 1931; Franklin D. Roosevelt elected president of United States, 1932; Vitamin C isolated and analyzed, 1932; Maytag advertised washing machine, 1932; Campbell's introduced tomato soup, 1932; Roosevelt launched his New Deal, 1933; Prohibition repealed, 1933; moral quality of motion pictures rated by Catholic Legion of Decency, 1934; federal Social Security Act passed, 1935;  Margaret Mitchell's bestselling novel, *Gone with the Wind*, published, 1936; Commercial production of nylon begun, 1938; television debut at New York World's Fair, 1939; Germany invaded Poland, bringing national unrest, 1939

# WINSOME MURMURS FROM THE 1930s

*There is as little snobbishness in the local Chapter of the Daughters of the American Revolution as in any other group…even though the membership can tell you who their Great-Aunt Susie's second husband's brother was. At their meeting on Tuesday the membership sat around during tea time discussing the ancestors whose valor entitles them to membership in this organization.*

*Not so long ago Dr. T.S. Bradfield, mayor of LaGrange, used to require young lawbreakers to pay fines as high as 75 cents and a dollar and to attend Sunday School in addition. In those days, it hurt to pay 75 cents, but it probably did the young blades even more good to be made to attend Sunday School.*

*Maybe teachers are believed to be more absent-minded than any other class of people. But what local preacher forgot his parked car and walked home twice in the same week?*

*Remember when pessimists said LaGrange would never be more than a one-horse town?*

*Remember when Broad Street was unpaved and the street department used to sprinkle it with oil to keep down the dust? Now it could do with a little dust to absorb the oil which drips from auto crankshafts.*

# Musings from America's Greatest Little City

*Toy trains apparently have a fascination for everybody, to judge by the varying ages of persons who may be seen throughout the day gazing into the window of Hudson Hardware Company, and following with their eyes the circuit of a small electric train.*

*There was rejoicing in the household of Dr. G.C. Hunter, LaGrange dentist, today following recovery of their Christmas turkey that disappeared from a mysteriously made hole in his coop two nights ago. The turkey was found wandering about the neighborhood on Wednesday, after having been given up for lost.*

## CHAPTER 6
# The 1940s

From *LaGrange Daily News*

The decade of the 1940s began with warning signals of increasing world unrest, concentrated in Europe and in the Far East.

The Selective Service Act had been signed by President Franklin Delano Roosevelt, and as a result, at home, LaGrange and Troup County men registered for the armed forces, beginning in 1940. Many draftees reported for active service in that year, according to the *Daily News*.

WLAG, LaGrange's first radio station, went on the air in 1941, giving the city another daily source of local and national news.

Before the first week in December 1941, the local daily was reporting, "The Far Eastern crisis appears to be growing more serious by the hour." Because the newspaper did not publish on Sunday, it missed a "scoop," and it was Monday, December 8, when the local newspaper's banner headline reported—what the whole world already knew—"United States Declares War."

"A Sunday attack on Pearl Harbor by Japan, left 3,000 casualties in Hawaii; 1500 people dead, two warships sunk, other ships damaged and a large number of Army and Navy airplanes out of commission," according to the newspaper's account of the history made on Sunday, December 7, 1941.

Further reporting revealed that on December 8, "within 20 minutes after President Roosevelt asked a joint session of Congress to do so, our nation declared war on Japan, following a U.S. Senate vote of 82 to nothing in favor." The vote in the House of Representatives was 388 to 1. The dissenting vote was cast by Representative Jeanette Rankin of Montana.

# Musings from America's Greatest Little City

In the eloquent message delivered to Congress at the Capitol on that occasion, including his "December 7 is a day that will live in infamy" statement, President Roosevelt added: "No matter how long it may take to overcome this premeditated invasion, the American people in their righteous might will win through to absolute victory."

On December 12, a headline in the *Daily News* read: "U.S. Answers Germany, Italy, with Prompt Declaration of War Today." Germany and Italy had declared war on the United States on December 11, and the U.S. Congress was unanimous in its answer—a vote that confirmed "a state of war exists between the U.S., Germany and Italy." This was in response to the president's written request to Congress for such action.

That same week, an editorial in the *News* revealed the writer's feelings:

> God help us when the war is over to be united in the determination that never again shall we be party to another conference of nations dedicated to disarmament in order to reach a balance of impotence among the nations. We are going to win this war. It may take years, but we will win the war, and when it is won, the destiny of the world will be in our hands. If we fail to remain strong in order to bring about and maintain a world of law, order and justice, we will have missed the boat for the last time and will deserve the fate that will befall us. Let us have all the idealistic peace talk possible—except that peace talk that would advocate balance of power when the war is over. If we fail to be in unity on that point when this conflict is over, the sacrifices and tears and blood will have been in vain.

Almost immediately headlines appeared in the *Daily News*, such as "America Is Now as One" and "How Much Can We Give?" These were followed by the news, "Local plans are being made to raise a 'Red Cross War Fund' expected to bring in $10,000 by noon on December 18." The goal was surpassed by that time, and on December 30, the newspaper reported that more than $20,000 had been raised, with more to come. In a late December report, it was noted that "employees of Dixie, Dunson and Callaway mills have contributed $16,403 to the Red Cross."

A portion of another December editorial in the *Daily News* should be shared with these war-time reports of LaGrange at this important time in its history. It read: "People of LaGrange have had ten days to consider the meaning of Pearl Harbor—crystallizing America's millions into a unity of purpose—that purpose being the eventual banishing of the double-crossing and criminal dictator-regimes from the world forever."

By December 30, the newspaper reported that the Civilian Defense Committee for Troup County, which had been organized in 1940, "has organized the city of LaGrange into 29 Defense Zones with volunteer wardens for each zone." Air raid and fire wardens were named, though in the report they had conceded that "chances are remote that we will experience air raids. In this war we must be prepared for every eventuality."

The home support of our servicemen and -women, even during the earliest days of the war, was magnificent and highly productive. News stories about the progress of the war and personal items about those away in service were reported daily.

Headlines appearing in the *News* attested to the all-out war effort being exerted locally. Examples like the following were appearing: "Citizens Bring Gifts for U.S.O. Christmas Tree"; "Atlanta Red Cross Bloodmobile Unit Here for Local Blood Drive for Troops"; "War Bonds and Stamps, Popular Christmas Gifts This Year"; "Callaway Armed Forces Center Sending Packages to Former Employees in Service"; "Pupils in LaGrange Schools Waging Warfare on Axis, Collecting Paper, Metal, Buying Bonds and Stamps"; "Troup County Ships 12 Carloads of Paper Needed in War"; and many more.

News that we had all dreaded to see came early in 1942. The *Daily News* reported that David Butler of West Point, who was serving in the navy, was the first Troup County serviceman to die in World War II. He died on February 24, 1942.

The days of World War II brought many changes in the day-to-day lives of LaGrange residents. With many family members and friends (both men and women) in the service, the folks at home helped the war effort by working in indispensable industries, volunteering in community and church projects, planting victory gardens, buying war bonds and stamps, participating in car pools and learning to live with and use the ration books issued by the government to control the purchasing of food items, tires, gasoline and shoes. The *Daily News* contained many stories supporting these efforts.

"In 1943, the Clubwomen of Troup County and Fulton County sold a sufficient amount of War Bonds to have a bomber named for the clubwomen and their counties," according to the *Daily News*. "Troup County sold the second largest amount of any county and Georgia clubwomen placed fourth in the nation in the amount of bonds sold."

Another highly successful local effort that involved many people was the collection of tin cans. The Junior Red Cross and students at LaGrange High School collected cans, and the LaGrange Fire Department prepared the cans for shipment. In May 1944, the *Daily News* reported, "170,954 tin cans have been collected by city and county schools, with Hogansville's report still to come." In August 1944, "14,635 pounds of waste paper have been collected."

The War Loan Drives were highly successful all during the war years. Just to mention one example, "Troup County's 7th War Loan Drive raised $2,294,817, exceeding its quota by $447,000," as reported in the *Daily News*.

Knowing it would be impossible to report the action of all of our local heroes, as the *Daily News* did, we will recognize only a few. Our selection should be understandable. All of these first items about men in the service appeared in the newspaper in 1944.

In March 1944, the fourth of four LaGrange brothers in the service, Cadet Robert Eugene Mann, was receiving pilot training at the Greenwood (Mississippi) Army Air Field. His brothers—Captain John M. Mann, Lieutenant Lowell K. Mann and Corporal Otis A. Mann—were already fighting in the war.

In July, Hal Webb Maley was reported as having been killed in action on June 24 in New Guinea. He was one of five brothers in the service—Staff Sergeant Roy H. Maley in France, Sergeant William H. Maley in Italy, Corporal John L. Maley in England and Private Hugh W. Maley (Hal's twin) at Camp Croft, South Carolina.

In August, Private First Class Harvey Gilbert was wounded in action and recovering in a hospital in England. He had three brothers in the service—Private Joseph Gilbert in the South Pacific, Sergeant Amos Gilbert at Keesler Field in Mississippi and Claude Eugene Gilbert in the United States Navy.

Troup County twins, both first class privates—Horace and Harold Todd of Hogansville—were awarded Combat Infantry badges for distinguished service on duty while under fire against the Japanese at Bougainville in September. Their older brother, James Todd, was reported to be with the United States Navy somewhere near the coast of Italy at that time.

In October 1944, the Reverend and Mrs. C.W. Hanson had six sons in the service. They were Seaman J.W. Hanson, at that time in St. Albans Hospital in New York, recovering from wounds received in the Normandy invasion; Aviator Machinist's Mate C.R. Hanson in the central Pacific; Corporal G.C. Hanson in France; Private Olin M. Hanson with the Air Corps in Colorado Springs, Colorado; Fireman C.C. Hanson, en route overseas; and Seaman J.E. Hanson at San Diego.

In December 1944, the Baxter L. Schaub Post No. 75 of the American Legion began a campaign to raise $50,000 for a new Legion home. The building would be a memorial to veterans of World War II who gave their lives for their country. "Space was planned for it to be a recreational center for returning veterans, who would be eligible for memberships," according to the announcement in the *Daily News*.

Up to this point, your chronicler has avoided any personal references to family and friends, but at this point it seems appropriate. There were many families in similar circumstances during the war; ours seemed to be typical. At the time that this writer was a sophomore at LaGrange College, she had a brother, Charles Franklin Traylor, in indispensable industry, building air bases and army hospitals; a brother, James Edward Traylor Jr., building bridges in Europe, for General Patton's forces, as a combat captain (later a major) in the Army Corps of Engineers; and two brothers-in-law, Thomas Lee Kincaid in the Coast Guard and Albert Louis Gelders in the United States Army Air Force.

In 1944, this Georgia girl received a letter from England, from the mother of a young RAF Spitfire pilot trained in Alabama and Georgia, with whom she had corresponded by V-Mail letters since 1942, after he had received his wings, returned home to England and was sent to North Africa. The letter reported that the mother's only son, RAF Flight Sergeant Thomas Peter Treleaven Oliver, had been killed in a crash near an air base at Castel Benito in North Africa. He was twenty-two and a half years old. He was buried in a British cemetery in Tripoli, Libya. A memorial tribute, published in a clipping from an English newspaper, enclosed with the letter, stated, "Only four of Peter's 24 classmates in college in Harrogate, Yorkshire, survived the war."

Peter's two sisters, Mary and Jean, married American soldiers who served in England; the brides came to live in Pennsylvania and Texas, respectively. After the war, the elder Olivers and their daughter Mary visited in the Dyar home in Georgia, and a strong friendship was formed between the families.

This same story, with different names, could have easily been reported by other Georgia families whose lives were enriched during the war by receiving young British RAF cadets into their homes while the boys were having their flight training in the States.

Leaving the personal, "typical family" memories, we found many more items in issues of the *Daily News* during this decade reporting the bravery and great service records of individuals from LaGrange and Troup County who served in World War II. These items would easily fill another book.

In January 1945, "LST Vessel No. 647 was commissioned at New Orleans, La., sponsored by a LaGrange firm, Daniel Lumber Company," as reported in the *Daily News*. The news item explained, "Sponsoring involves providing recreational and other equipment for the comfort and recreation of the officers and men in the ship's crew. The commanding officer of the vessel was Lt. R. Howard O'Neal of LaGrange, in the USNR."

There were many women from LaGrange and Troup County who served in the armed forces with distinction during World War II. Six of these were mentioned in the following articles in the *News*, three in June 1944 and three in January and February 1945.

In June 1944, Mrs. Frances C. Miner, a seaman first class in the WAVES, had been assigned to duty in the personnel office of the Naval Air Station in Atlanta. Her husband, Corporal James P. Miner, was in the army serving somewhere in the South Pacific, and her brother, Harold Carlisle, was in the army in New Guinea. At that same time, Mildred V. Peach, pharmacist's mate second class with the WAVES, was on duty in the nursing dispensary as nurse and laboratory assistant with the U.S. Naval Station at Dallas, Texas. She had a brother, Frank J. Peach, also in the navy, and a sister, Second Lieutenant Martha A. Peach, in the Army Nurses Corp.

In January 1945, Mary Strickland Reeder was a private in the Women's Army Corps taking her basic training at the Third WAC Training Center in Fort Oglethorpe, Georgia. Her husband, Private Bert Reeder was in the infantry somewhere in the South Pacific, and her brother, Sergeant Cecil Strickland, was in the Army Air Force in France.

In February, WAC Corporal Virginia C. Little of West Point was serving in the Netherlands East Indies in the office of the chief surgeon, U.S. Army Services, and Clovis Todd was reporting for induction as a lieutenant in the Army Nurses Corps in Camp Rucker, Alabama.

In bringing this service report to a conclusion, we include this *Daily News* story from November 1945 about a memorial service sponsored by members of the local post of the American Legion and held between halves at the LaGrange High School–Cedartown football game to honor LHS students who gave their lives in World War II. The names listed were:

*John Bolden, Hanley Burson, Ralph Cole, Hugh Chitwood, Lonza Claxton, L.Z. Crowe, William Dean, Cleaveland Evans, George Eiland, Marvin Folds, Charles Graham, George Jackson, William McCluskey, Robert Neeley, William Norris, Sig Owen Jr., Thomas Payne, Allen Pittman, Emmett Skelton, Fred Still, Ed Voorhees, Fred Whaley, and Douglas White.*

Dr. S.C. Rutland, commander of the local Legion post, announced that the list could be incomplete, "since records of the school were destroyed in a fire that razed the building several years ago." The name of Boyd Carver, listed at that time as missing in action on Okinawa, was added in a later issue of the *Daily News*.

"In April, 1945, the entire nation mourned the death of President Franklin D. Roosevelt, who died while on a visit to Warm Springs, Georgia," as reported in the *Daily News*. A funeral train carried his body to Washington; memorial services were held in LaGrange and throughout the country. Burial was at Hyde Park, New York. Messages of sympathy and praise for this exceptional war-time leader were received from many parts of the world. News reports told us "simple services were held at the White House, as houses of Parliament are closed in England, and Russians pay highest tribute to U.S. President. Thousands line streets in Washington, as the world honors Roosevelt today [April 14]. Vice President Harry S. Truman began his duties as our nation's 32nd chief executive immediately."

At that same time, the *News* was predicting "Collapse of Germany Imminent," with a further statement: "These are the final hours for Hitler's Germany." And, almost immediately in the *Daily News*, people were being urged to "have a sane V-E Day in LaGrange, attending church." This item continued: "When V-E Day comes, there will be no drinking or rowdiness in LaGrange. All beer joints in town must close for 24 hours, and people are urged to attend some church service for prayers and thanksgiving, according to an order issued by Mayor R.S. O'Neal."

The Nazis surrendered on May 8, and V-E Day was declared by the United States, Britain and Russia. Fighting ceased at 6:00 p.m.

The time had come for thanksgiving and celebration in LaGrange and everywhere in the free world! The *Daily News* story read: "At 8 o'clock this morning two whistles blew long blasts to notify LaGrange residents that V-E Day has come at last. This morning at 11 o'clock, services were held in churches in LaGrange, and all stores and offices in LaGrange were closed for the hour. Special thanksgiving services were held at every public school and at LaGrange College."

President Truman quickly reminded the nation, "Victory Is But Half Won." In a statement published immediately in our local daily, as well as in others, "The President calls upon all Americans to stick to posts until battle is won." Two other headlines that same day read "War as Usual in Pacific" and "Allied Troops Moving from Europe to Pacific Theater."

In June 1945, the *Daily News* reported, "86th Division Comes Home En Route to War in Pacific." The news item announced, "A LaGrange boy, Sgt.

Harvey Haynes, employee of Hillside Plant of Callaway Mills before he entered service, was the first Georgia boy down the gang-plank in New York. He was with the 341st Regiment, First Battalion Headquarters Company."

The campaign in the Pacific was gaining momentum every day, and there was bad news for Japan all along that battlefront. General Eisenhower was welcomed home "in a 38-mile parade, with millions crowding streets of New York." All this was reported in the *Daily News*.

In August, President Truman addressed the nation and "the secret of Oak Ridge was out, after three years." Oak Ridge, Tennessee, was revealed, according to the news report, "as one of the production centers for the new, deadly atom bombs." At this time, President Truman announced that "an American plane had loosed one of the new bombs on the important Japanese army base at Hiroshima."

Tokyo Radio's response was: "The destructive power of the new weapon cannot be slighted. The devastation from this one atomic bomb was so great that authorities still have not ascertained the full extent of it."

More news reports came—"Japanese Under Merciless Attacks as Allies Lash Enemy Islands in Withering Land, Sea, Air Battles." Nagasaki had been "slashed by atomic power," and the Russians were "hurling a million troops into the Japanese fight."

The end of war with Japan came soon after these developments, later in August. Local coverage in the *Daily News* read like this:

> *LaGrange is celebrating the greatest victory it has ever known—the end of the war with a nation that swore it would bring us crumbling to our knees. This is the second half end, of the scourge that has left its imprint on our minds for generations to come. Last night Court Square was bedlam. Main Street was in chaos. Everywhere the city was in an uproar. And still LaGrange is literally "blowing its top." Mayor R.S. O'Neal urged all citizens to attend some religious services and in every other appropriate manner show evidence of sincere thankfulness from our hearts for the victory gained by our fighting men and women. May God grant them a safe return to their homes here and elsewhere in this beloved nation.*

By October, the newspaper was reporting the arrival home of many war veterans who had served many months and, in some cases, even years, of duty overseas.

It was reported that month that the Veterans of Foreign Wars State Extension Office had received the application and charter fee for a local

VFW charter, opening the way for a LaGrange post. The newspaper account added, "The recently organized post includes veterans who have served in three major wars—the Spanish American War and World Wars I and II. The youngest member is Pfc. William Breed, 18-year-old Marine, now serving somewhere in the Pacific."

In December 1945, the Albert J. Perry Post of the Veterans of Foreign Wars sponsored a memorial service for Lieutenant Albert J. Perry, who was killed in action with the Eighth Air Force over Germany. The service was held at the Southwest LaGrange Baptist Church, according to the *Daily News*. In August 1945, the paper had reported that Lieutenant Perry, the pilot of a B-17, had been missing over Germany since August 16 of that year. A death report had followed. His brother, Private First Class J.C. Perry, also served in the Army Air Force. Later in the decade of the 1940s, this VFW group made plans to build a home for their post, which had been named in memory of the young pilot.

As Christmas was approaching, the newspaper reported, "Santa Claus, the roly-poly fellow with the chubby cheeks and twinkling eyes, is all thumbs this year. It is because of the changeover from wooden toys of the war years to the new metal and mechanical toys. Santa has been out of practice for quite a while now, and it seems he just can't seem to work a screw driver fast enough."

"In February of 1946, Mrs. Clarence Crisp, the 20-year-old English bride of a LaGrange GI, was one of 1700 British wives who landed in New York aboard the Queen Mary, to join their husbands in all sections of the United States," according to the *Daily News*. Clarence Crisp had served with the U.S. Army in the European Theater of Operations for three years. In the account of his bride's arrival in the states, she was quoted as saying, "Americans are so friendly and there is so much food here." LaGrange and Troup County were fortunate to have other young war brides like Mrs. Crisp joining their husbands after the war.

The war dominated the news columns of the local paper in the first half of the 1940s, but other items of interest were covered, as well. An important story in October 1946 reported, "LaGrange High School's new, sprawling, limestone building has now been completed, taking the place of the brick structure on North Greenwood Street, which was burned." The fire had occurred on December 26, 1942. After the old Harwell Avenue School building used briefly by the high school students was destroyed by fire in 1943, students attended classes in the Sunday school building of the First Methodist Church from 1943 until 1946, when the new building was completed.

"The new high school was constructed at a cost of approximately $450,000 and the equipment cost was estimated at about $75,000." The enrollment in October 1946 was "approximately 600 students," as reported in the *Daily News*, in the same write-up about the building, which was believed at that time "to be one of the most modern high school buildings in the entire South."

In the dedicatory address for the building, the speaker, Hubert T. Quillian, president of LaGrange College, said: "The new high school stands as a symbol of the obligation that each generation has to impart its treasures of wisdom and knowledge to the generation that follows. It is formally dedicated to the promotion of the principles of democracy and the love of liberty, a knowledge of truth, and the acquisition of understanding and wisdom."

In December 1947, a report was sent from Nuremberg, Germany, to Georgia by Ralph McGill, editor of the *Atlanta Constitution*, and it was quoted in the *Daily News*: "Judge Lee B. Wyatt of LaGrange is making a fine reputation as a presiding judge at the War Crimes Trials. Judge Wyatt's court is far ahead of the other courts in progress of the cases." Editor McGill also reported

The second LaGrange High School building, completed on a new site in 1915. It was destroyed by fire in 1942. A new building on the same site opened in 1946.

that Judge and Mrs. Wyatt were in good health but were eager to get back to their home in LaGrange. Judge Wyatt had been appointed to serve by President Truman. When appointed, he said he had "accepted the post because he knew he would be serving his nation and humanity."

In January and February 1948, plans were being made for the completion of a project, proposed in 1941 as a memorial to the builders of LaGrange and Troup County. "Original plans for a fountain and park on the Square had been delayed because of the war, and the commandeering of all materials for the war effort," according to the *Daily News*. Contributions to the memorial fund had been made in 1941 by hundreds of men and women, boys and girls. Approximately $34,000 in cash had been raised at that time. Cost of construction had more than doubled in the intervening years. In January 1948, Hal N. Brady Jr., president of the LaGrange Chamber of Commerce, announced, "Bids have been received and total cost, including materials and landscaping for an electrical fountain and park will be $61,849.46."

Citizens contributed the additional funds needed to meet the increase in the cost of the project. Daniel Lumber Company was the low bidder for construction costs, and Southern Landscape Service of Covington, as low bidder, was awarded the contract for landscaping. In February, the newspaper announced, "Work will begin as soon as weather conditions permit, and completion can be expected by early summer."

A legal "hitch" developed, as reported in the *Daily News* in March, and it was June before the details had been worked out and an agreement reached to the satisfaction of all parties involved so that work on the park could begin. The *News* reported, "LaGrange may now look forward to the benefits and beauty of this important civic improvement."

In September, completion of the park was expected by the end of December, weather permitting. The fountain, with colored lights, was at that time under construction.

Two important events, bringing many visitors to town, occurred in March 1949. "More than 600 visitors from 13 states and one foreign country registered during the tour of the century-old gardens at Hills and Dales, the home of Mr. and Mrs. Fuller E. Callaway Jr., who opened the gardens for the benefit of the building fund of St. Mark's Episcopal Church," according to a report in the *Daily News*. In that same month, the city dedicated the new LaGrange–Troup County Memorial Park on the square, which had been vacant since the courthouse burned in 1936. The *Daily News* reported its dedication on March 31: "More than 5,000 men and women, boys and girls of LaGrange and Troup

County, have given the funds to erect the park as a memorial to the builders of the city and county. The park has a handsome fountain, lighted in colors at night, and it is beautifully landscaped and planted with shrubs and grass."

The *Daily News* reported a "first" for LaGrange in August 1949, when "LaGrange's own Miss Dorothy Johnston was chosen 'Miss Georgia 1949' at the State Pageant held in Columbus. The 18-year-old beauty, who is seeking an operatic career, will represent Georgia in the Miss America Pageant to be held in Atlantic City in early September. For her talent in Columbus, Miss Johnston sang a portion of Sempre Libre from the opera, 'La Traviata.'"

## MOSAIC MUSINGS FROM THE 1940S

*The Gallup Poll has found that one adult in four believes television will doom radio. Those who share this opinion probably predicted back in the 1920s that radio would doom the phonograph. Instead, they got married and parented the radio-phonograph. Our prediction, if you're interested, is that TV will marry the offspring.*

*Five LaGrange women, motoring from Atlanta in 1947, reported seeing a "flying saucer" making its way through the clouds between East Point and Fairburn. The witnesses all agree that the encounter was exciting. They watched the object, a bright silver disc, for about ten minutes until it seemed to disappear into thin air when they were nearly to Fairburn.*

That same year, in a national news item in the *Daily News*:

*The Army Air Force is continuing the aerial hunt for those little "saucers" that aren't there—or are they? No one seems to know. But the Army isn't taking any chances. It is sending up a fleet of camera-equipped planes to hunt down those mysterious objects which have been flashing before the eyes of many citizens.*

## OPENINGS/FOUNDINGS

Troup County Home Defense formed, 1940; LaGrange Housing Authority, 1941; Congregation Beth-El, 1945; Mutual Concert Series, 1945; new LaGrange High School, 1946; National Guard unit, Forty-eighth Cavalry mechanized reconnaissance troop, 1947; new clubhouse for Highland Country Club, 1948; new bus station, 1948; West Georgia Cancer Clinic, 1948; Girl Scouts "Little House," 1948; Civil Air Patrol, 1949

## ORGANIZATIONS

LaGrange Kiwanis Club chartered, 1941; Veterans of Foreign Wars Auxiliary, 1946; Troup County Hereford Association, 1946; Perry Post of American Legion, 1946; Negro American Legion Post, 1949; LaGrange Real Estate Board, 1949

## HAPPENINGS

Troup County males registered for national conscription, first draftees left, 1940; war declared on Japan, Germany and Italy, 1941; LaGrange High School building destroyed by fire, 1942; dedication of new Callaway Auditorium, 1942; LaGrange Woman's Club received Bellevue as gift from Fuller E. Callaway Foundation, 1942; Troup County exceeded bond quotas,

Callaway Auditorium, built in 1942. Callaway Foundation, Inc., gave this building to LaGrange College in 1992.

Bellevue, Confederate senator Benjamin Harvey Hill's home, was built in the mid-1850s. It was a gift to the LaGrange Woman's Club from the Fuller E. Callaway Foundation in 1942.

1945 and 1948; LaGrange College accredited by Southern Association of Colleges on first application, 1946; City-County Hospital addition bonds passed, 1947; natural gas reached LaGrange, 1947; water bond issue passed, 1948; St. Mark's Episcopal Church in new building, 1949; Render Apartments destroyed by fire, 1949; Miss Dorothy Johnston named "Miss Georgia" in state pageant, 1949

# 1940s Decade Review—Nationally

Selective Service Act signed, 1940; Japanese attacked Pearl Harbor, 1941; U.S. declared war on Japan, Germany and Italy, 1941; television broadcasting began in United States, 1941; food rationing, 1942; streptomycin discovered, 1943; GI Bill of Rights enacted, 1944; penicillin on market, 1944; President Franklin D. Roosevelt took oath of office for fourth time, 1945; President Roosevelt died and Vice President Harry S. Truman sworn in as president, 1945; U.S. drops atomic bomb on Japan, 1945; World War II ended with victories in Europe and Japan, 1945; horrors of Nazi concentration camps exposed, 1945; United Nations established with United States a charter member, 1945; first computer introduced, 1946; cortisone development announced, 1946; the Reverend Billy Graham began his evangelistic career, 1946; sugar rationing ended, 1947; living costs hit highest peak in nation's history, 1947; teaching religious education in public schools declared unconstitutional by Supreme Court, 1948; WSB-TV first television station in Georgia, 1948; electric dishwashers introduced by KitchenAid, 1949

# WINSOME MURMURS FROM THE 1940s

*Filler: Hitler passed up a chance to make a radio talk the other day* [in 1944]. *It must have dawned on even "Der Furious" that no one is listening to him anymore.*

*Hitler has just decorated two German field marshals, defeated on the Russian front. Since when has he been awarding consolation prizes?*

*Filler: English and American novelists, in 1944, are trying to find the most beautiful words in the language. That's easy! They are, "I quit," as spoken by a certain Adolf Hitler.*

*Eleanor's Letter: During one of the tense moments of the movie yesterday at the LaGrange Theater, an elderly gentleman began groping for something on the floor, greatly disturbing the lady in the next seat. "What have you lost?" she asked testily. "A caramel," answered the man. "You're going to all of this bother for a measly caramel," she asked. "Yes," was his reply, "my teeth are in it."*

*Bachelor girls, you can stop twiddling your thumbs and get that fourth finger on your left hand in a receptive mood. The government, in 1947, has brought the official word, through the Census Bureau, that the shortage of bachelors is over.*

*Eleanor's Letter: The pet shows that the Callaway Education Association has been sponsoring this week have created quite a stir among the animals of LaGrange. The various playgrounds have looked like so many menageries during the shows. What has the judges stymied, however, is how Roy East of the Calumet playground, ever managed to get his cow dressed up in overalls, shirt, blue and white striped tie and blue hat. But "Bossie" was contented with her lot, and didn't let out a whimper.*

*Mr. Groundhog: Better stay in bed! It's cold outside. Any groundhog that gets out of his warm bed tomorrow is a danged fool! The country is half covered with snow, and the other half is shivering. The weatherman says it is cold.*

*New York Goes Bathless and Shaveless 24 Hours—Officials have put the city of New York's eight million residents on their honor today* [December 16, 1949] *to go "Shaveless and Bathless" for the next 24 hours to save water.*

## CHAPTER 7
# The 1950s

From *LaGrange Daily News*

While LaGrange was enjoying prosperity in the decade of the 1950s, recurring topics seemed to take the greater amount of space in the news and editorial columns in the local daily. These topics were religion, the Korean War, educational changes and the onset of "football fever" in local sports fans.

In January 1950, an editorial in the *Daily News* brought comments on a national trend that was welcome news in our hometown:

> *Rock of Ages—One of the most notable events in postwar America has been the striking revival of interest in religion. It has shown itself in many ways, but mostly in record attendance at church and a vast consumption of inspirational books. It has been a quest for certainty amid a flood of confusion and doubt. It has been a spontaneous response, a fulfillment of need.*

An editorial in August 1952 addressed the subject of religion with the headline, "Church Rolls at Peak," informing "those persons, whose one service in life is to extol that the world is 'going to the dogs,' that they will be surprised to hear from good authority that the church rolls in the United States have reached a new peak."

In the *Yearbook of the American Churches*, edited by Dr. Benson Y. Landis, it was announced that "religious congregations in the United States had a total of 88,673,005 members at the end of 1951." The local editor expressed his thoughts on this news: "We feel that the increasing church rolls, reflected here

First Presbyterian Church, Broad Street, 1921. It was restored in 1953 at the same site after a 1951 fire. The earlier building on Church Street is now the property of Covenant Presbyterian Church.

in LaGrange, are encouraging to those who are trying to better themselves, their city and their country."

Other editorial comments on religion in this decade stressed the national increase in church membership with supporting documented statistics. A *Newsweek* magazine survey in 1955 stated that "30 years ago Protestants totaled 27 percent of the population. Today they exceed 35 percent, taking into consideration the increase in population." The LaGrange editor added his own comments when he wrote, "While church membership itself is not a guarantee of a good life, at least, they're headed in the right direction."

In LaGrange and in the county, church congregations were growing as part of this national trend. New churches were being established; others were reporting expansions because of increased membership. In downtown LaGrange in the 1950s, the largest churches were often in the news.

On April 29, 1951, the First Presbyterian Church building on Broad Street was destroyed by fire. Sunday morning services were held in the LaGrange High School for two years, according to reports in the *Daily News*. A story in February 1953 announced: "An imposing new building for the First Presbyterian Church in LaGrange, raised at a cost of $305,567, has replaced the old church building, which burned in 1951. Money for the new structure was raised by members and by generous gifts from others of all denominations. During the building program, a manse for the pastor was erected on Pineview Terrace."

St. Mark's Episcopal Church was consecrated by Bishop John B. Walthour of the Atlanta Diocese on August 10, 1952. At that time the *Daily News* reported the event, adding this further information: "According to a canon law of the Episcopal Church, a consecration service by the congregation of a church marks the payment of all indebtedness on the church, which was completed in 1949. St. Mark's was originally organized as a parish-house on Easter Sunday in 1864, with 31 communicants."

Later in the decade, the newspaper reported that on April 25, 1955, a chapel was dedicated at St. Mark's "memorializing the Holy Comforter Mission which was formerly located on Stonewall Street. The chapel will be used for private devotionals, communion and small weddings."

A major renovation of the sanctuary of First Baptist Church in LaGrange began in June 1955 as the final phase of the complete remodeling of the church. The *Daily News* reported, "The remodeled sanctuary, a gift to the church from Mr. and Mrs. Fuller E. Callaway Jr., will be completed in about four months and will include a new treatment of the front exterior of the building, bringing new front entrances on the ground floor." The report added that a new eight-room home for the pastor and his family had been completed in December.

First Baptist Church on the Square. This card, dated in the late 1890s, precedes many renovations. The building has been greatly enlarged through years and now has six columns, a steeple and a new sanctuary.

The First United Methodist Church was often in the *News* with reports on its activities, but its "big news story" was to come in 1964, on the completion of its new sanctuary on its original site.

Many LaGrange women from the various denominations were members of the LaGrange Council of Church Women. On September 13, 1955, the *Daily News* announced that the council had "opened a used clothing center in rooms above Funderburk Auto Supply Company on East Court Square. The center will be open for two hours on Tuesday afternoons and two hours on Thursday mornings. The center will be operated by a committee of volunteers named by the Council. All donations will be used for needy families in the city."

Immediately after the South Korean capital of Seoul fell to the Communists on June 28, 1950, Mayor Duke Davis of LaGrange made a request of local citizens on the front page of the *Daily News*:

> *A Proclamation—I hereby proclaim the week of June 28 to July 5, a week of prayer for "Divine guidance in behalf of our national leaders in dealing with the impending crisis in Korea." As a reminder to our people to go to prayer, I earnestly request that the church bells be rung at noon each day; that this proclamation be carried in the LaGrange Daily News, along with a paragraph on the "Power of Prayer," each day, from one of our local ministers.*

In July 1950, an editorial in the *Daily News* helped local readers understand what our nation was facing after our troops were sent to defend South Korea. The writer said:

> *We Must Win—Every day it becomes more and more apparent that we are not fighting a mere police action in Korea, and that it will not be over in one week or two. It behooves us, therefore, to make some immediate long-range plans so that we may better cope with the situation. Our economy will be threatened and there will be those who say "we can't win" in the face of all this, but our determination must be as strong as our heritage. We must begin now to develop the "victor's complex" that has always permeated our leaders and our forces. If it's a life and death struggle with Communist aggression, we must win it.*

In August 1950, the local draft board announced in the newspaper, "75 men were called up and 52 were chosen from that number for pre-induction examinations for service."

The first death notice of a LaGrange boy killed in action in Korea was published in the *Daily News* on September 7, 1950. It announced that "Pfc. Grover Thomas, 20, was killed in action August 31, while serving with the First Marine Division in Korea."

This was quickly followed by many military reports providing local citizens with war news of great interest and concern. Another item came later that same month about Master Sergeant Billie E. Zimmerman of Hogansville, who had been awarded the Silver Star medal for "gallantry in action against the enemy on September 12, while a member of the United States First Cavalry Division in Korea."

By February 1951, the local daily was reporting many medals and awards to local servicemen, including two more Silver Stars. Private First Class Alton T. Johnson of LaGrange had been cited for gallantry on September 17, 1950, and was reported missing in action the following day. His parents received his Silver Star in his name. The second one, reported at that time, was for Sergeant Bobby L. Woodruff, a private first class in a tank battalion at the time he received his citation for gallantry in action on January 28, 1951.

In August 1951, a report was published in the *News* concerning the "Final Rites for Three LaGrange Soldiers" that read: "Funeral services for three LaGrange servicemen, who gave their lives for this country, will be held tomorrow. Legionnaire riflemen will fire a final salute over the graves of each soldier in their final rites." The three were Sergeant Rudy Bud Smith, Corporal James R. Rosamond Jr. and Private First Class Alton T. Johnson, the MIA mentioned in an earlier report about his parents' receiving his Silver Star in his name.

Also in 1951, the *Daily News* reported that "an Army doctor from LaGrange, Captain William G. Avery, is now serving as a surgeon in Korea with the 8055th Mobile Army Surgical Hospital (MASH), a revolutionary milestone in military medicine."

An announcement from the United States Army published in the *News* in June 1952 reported that "a bridge in Korea had been named for a LaGrange soldier, Cpl. Vernon D. Hyde, who was killed while clearing a mine field. The commanding officer of Hyde's unit, the 1343rd Engineer Combat Battalion, dedicated the bridge in a ceremony with Hyde's former comrades participating." Funeral services were held for Corporal Hyde at Dunson Baptist Church in LaGrange in June, after his body was returned to the States, according to a later newspaper report.

These items about local and county servicemen were followed by many others printed in this decade, some reporting injuries, some deaths, some missing in actions, as well as many of the happy kind, announcing the return of many of our heroes of the war to the Seattle port of embarkation under the army's rotation program for Korean veterans.

An example of the happy reports was one in the *Daily News* in May 1953, when Private Floyd Philpott was "greeted with a rousing welcome as Hogansville turned out in full force to greet her hometown hero, home again after two years in a Chinese Communist prisoner-of-war camp. Philpott was the sixth American and the first Georgian to be released by the Reds. The 24-year-old private first class said to the assembled hometown crowd, 'I know your prayers pulled me through.'"

In October 1953, the *Daily News* brought the good news that "LaGrange and Troup County had turned out October 1, to pay tribute to Captain Joseph H. Hearn, returned Air Force officer who was a prisoner of the Chinese Communists for more than two years." The twelve-year Air Force veteran of two wars, a radio operator, was shot down in a B-29 bombing raid over the Yalu River on April 12, 1951, and was reported missing in action. He was a prisoner of the Reds until September 3, 1953. An estimated crowd of three thousand people was on hand for the welcome home parade, according to the *Daily News*, and attended the ceremony that "paid tribute to his service and that of hundreds of other young men who have gone out from our county to serve this country in the Korean and in other wars."

A LaGrange mother of a serviceman made the news in this decade, as reported in the *Daily News*:

> *Mrs. H.F. Jarrell breathed a sigh of happy accomplishment a few days ago when she made the final stitches on two flags of the Republic of China to be sent to her youngest son, Captain Henry Jarrell, who is now with the United States Navy in Formosa, where the provincial government of the Chinese Republic is located. Captain Jarrell will present the flags to the Chinese Republic on October 10, an anniversary of its establishment over forty years ago. Captain Jarrell, a graduate of the United States Naval Academy, served in China about five years, during which time he studied the Chinese language. After three years out of the service, he was recalled to active duty and assigned to the naval base on Southern Formosa. "Henry asked me to make two flags," Mrs. Jarrell explained, "because the Chinese always make gifts in pairs. Pairs represent tranquility, unity and peace to them; a single gift represents discord, strife and war."*

Through the years, LaGrange citizens have been known for their patriotic spirit and generous support of all national defense efforts. A banner headline in July 1951 in the *Daily News* read "LaGrange, First in State to Receive Defense Bond Flag." The story continued:

> *In addition to being the first in the state, LaGrange is the third city in the entire Southeast, and the twenty-third city in the nation, to achieve the distinction of receiving this special flag. The Defense Bond Flag is given to cities where 80 percent or more of its employees are given the opportunity of buying Defense Bonds through the Payroll Savings Plan. More than 84 percent of the workers in LaGrange are helping in the defense of the nation in this way. The flag will be flown from the LaGrange Post Office.*

In January 1952, the *Daily News* reported that Troup County had 1,531 boys in the Armed Forces. In the same issue there was more news about bond sales—"Troup County residents have purchased $1,200,417 in Defense Bonds; $417 more than their goal."

From the earliest days, LaGrange has been recognized for its outstanding schools ranging from the elementary to the college levels of instruction.

In April 1950, LaGrange voters passed a $1,400,000 bond issue in a referendum that was reported in the *Daily News*: "Architects are at work on plans for the enlargement and improvement of many LaGrange school facilities. The expansion program includes five new grammar schools, new construction at two junior high schools, a new high school and new sanitary plumbing at another grammar school."

LaGrange citizens were gratified to read in an April 1952 *Daily News* that a Reviewing Committee from the Office of Education of the Federal Agency in Washington, D.C., had visited local schools and reported, "The LaGrange public school system can easily become a model for the entire state."

In May, after its visit to Troup County schools, the *News* reported that the committee, composed of prominent out-of-county educators, had "urged the replacement of most of the county's school buildings, as soon as funds are available."

In September 1952, the *Daily News* reported that Troup County had bought land near the city limits of LaGrange on the Whitesville road, on which "they will build a county-wide high school for rural students." It was further reported, "This school will house approximately 500 students and have the very latest in equipment and school programs."

In July 1953, the *News* reported that county schools were "to get building funds from bond sales to make possible the building of permanent-type schoolhouses to replace the present dilapidated frame buildings currently housing the county's school program." At that time, the Georgia School Building Authority had voted to release a Troup County quota of $1.7 million to be used in construction of two county high schools and eight county elementary schools.

Groundbreaking exercises for Troup County High School were held in December 1955, according to a *Daily News* story. This would "mark the beginning of construction of nine Troup County building projects being financed by the Georgia School Building Authority." On April 22, 1956, an open house for the new TCHS was announced in the *News*. Students had been attending classes in the new building for two months at that time. The state authority had provided $329,000 for the erection of the building. This open house announcement in the *News* also stated, "Equipment for the building was purchased from funds totaling $100,000 donated by Callaway Community Foundation of LaGrange."

On the college educational level, the big news from LaGrange College was announced in the *Daily News* in 1953: "The historic liberal arts institution is now officially coeducational." Male students had attended college classes in earlier decades, but they began receiving degrees in the 1950s. This development also brought sports news about the college's basketball and baseball teams, as well as announcements of new construction—a men's dormitory, Turner Hall, in the spring of 1958, and a modern gymnasium and physical education building, ready for occupation in February 1959.

It wasn't too great a surprise to LaGrange football fans in November 1953 when an editorial in the *Daily News* read: "Wish We Had a Stadium for Our Football Games—We have seen what LaGrange can do when we want to, and now we should want to build a new stadium for football play—as a start to a modern recreational facility for our city. It would show we have faith in the future of our young people. We should aim in that direction." At the time this editorial was written, the old sports stadium was being used more often for baseball games.

Other editorials in 1953 on the subject of sports saluted individual players and coaches on football teams in LaGrange, Hogansville and West Point, all of which were "on a roll" in the 1950s.

Coaches cited in the *Daily News* in 1953 were LaGrange coaches Oliver Hunnicutt and Al Mariotti; Russ Slaughter and James Hudson in Hogansville; and Carlton Lewis and Jack Creswell in West Point.

Front-page news in November 1958 brought this headline: "Foundation to Build Modern Football Stadium." An announcement followed that the Callaway Community Foundation was going to build a $250,000 football stadium in LaGrange; the facilities at the old Callaway Stadium were to be razed, and the new arena was to be located on the same site.

Plans were to allow the LaGrange and Troup County schools to use the stadium for their football games free of charge and to make the stadium available on a rental basis for other activities of interest to LaGrange citizens.

In July 1959, the *Daily News* reported that "the busiest place in town is the new Callaway Football Stadium." This was followed in September by this story:

*Stadium, Game Bring Glee to Football Fans—LaGrange showed appreciation last night when her citizens came out en masse at the first game to be played in the new 5,104-seat stadium, overflowing with football fans eager to see both the new stadium and Georgia's AAA 1958 champions test their mettle against the Lanett AA champions in Alabama. The LHS Grangers won 15–0.*

# MOSAIC MUSINGS FROM THE 1950s

*For 300 years the date of Thanksgiving has shuttled back and forth between July 30 and December 13. Up until recent years it was the last Thursday in November. Regardless of the date, it is a day set apart on which we give our thanks to almighty God for all His goodness and loving kindness to us. We, in LaGrange, live in a community that is set apart in this state as a wonderful place in which to live. So we should express our heartfelt gratitude to an all-glorious God who came to earth for our redemption. Yes, let us count our blessings.*

*The other day in Piccadilly Circus, the Broadway of London, England, three young soldiers from LaGrange met, had their pictures made together and enjoyed talking about home. The three are Pfc. Alfred Johnson, Sgt. Lamar Jones and Pfc. Jimmie D. Tucker. The three soldiers discovered that they are stationed within twenty miles of each other in England.*

*Santa Claus is going to pick up Sgt. Charles Waller of LaGrange and give him a 2,500-mile, free-ride home for Christmas dinner. The Sergeant, just back in California after 16 months as a fighting Marine in Korea, needed transportation and a pass for home when LaGrange Mayor Duke Davis, one of Santa's helpers, heard of the Marine's plight. With the help of U.S. Senator Dick Russell's Washington office, the Mayor arranged for the pass. Santa, fresh out of reindeer, decided an airliner would serve as well. So Sgt. Waller will wing his way home free, courtesy of an airliner. He'll land in Georgia and "be at home in LaGrange to sing the first chorus of 'Jingle Bells' on Christmas Eve," Santa promised.*

*R.T. "Mac" McClure can be blamed if golfers have to start buying hunting licenses. Yesterday, "Mac" killed a squirrel with a golf ball on number four hole at the Highland Country Club in LaGrange. He has witnesses to prove it. He was playing with George Ashmore, Roy Davidson, Loeb Ketzky and Horace Richter.*

*A B-29 super-fortress airplane paid a belated visit to the LaGrange-Callaway Airport yesterday. It was the first time one of the giant planes, America's best bomber in World War II, had landed at the local airport, built originally as an auxiliary field for the giant planes in 1944. The plane was on a test flight from the Lockheed plant in Marietta, Georgia, and settled down here after weather closed in on the Atlanta and Marietta airports. The landing proved quite a sensation to LaGrange residents, who rushed to their front porches and lawns when the deafening roar of the big plane rushed across the sky.*

*An ex–truck driver with sideburns and a motion like a good broken-field-running halfback is well on his way to establishing a new attendance record for a movie at the LaGrange Theater. The flashy "phenom," of course, is Elvis Presley. O.A. Cooper, manager of the local theater, says that if the present turnout trend continues, the movie, "Love Me Tender," will set a box-office record for his theater. The movie opened Sunday and will run through Wednesday, but, according to Cooper, will probably be held over.*

# OPENINGS/FOUNDINGS

LaGrange Council of Church Women's Clothing Center, 1955; Coleman Library, 1955; new National Guard Armory, 1955; Troup County High School, 1956; "The Harbor" (home for Christian rehabilitation of alcoholics), 1956

## ORGANIZATIONS

Ladies Elks Auxiliary, 1950; Negro Farm Bureau, 1950; Little League Baseball, 1952; Ladies Golf Association, 1955; LaGrange-area chapter of Georgia Association for Retarded Children, 1955

## HAPPENINGS

City mail deliveries cut to one per day, 1950; half-million-dollar storm damage, March 1950; city hired first city manager, 1950; Pepperell, Inc., bought Dunson Mills, 1950; dedication of Maidee Smith Memorial Nursery for Negro Children, 1951; LaGrange College became officially coeducational, 1953; Troup County women began serving on juries, 1954; open house for restored Bellevue, 1955; voters approved bond issue for hospital expansion, 1956; Congressional resolution introduced to study West Point Dam construction, 1957; STAR teacher and student program instituted locally, 1957; new Moose Lodge dedicated, 1957; new building completed for Clark-Holder Clinic, 1958; hula-hoop craze in LaGrange, 1958; new police/jail building, 1958

## 1950s DECADE REVIEW—NATIONALLY

United States sent troops to defend South Korea, 1950; General Dwight D. Eisenhower elected president, 1952; more than six million Americans owned stock, 1952; age of television arrived with more Americans buying sets, 1953; increased use of computers in industry, 1953; compulsory segregation in public schools ruled unconstitutional by Supreme Court, 1954; "One Nation Under God" added to Pledge of Allegiance to flag, 1954; polio vaccine found effective, 1955; "In God We Trust" added to American currency, 1955; road-building projects provided by Congressional Interstate Highway Bill, 1956; Asian flu epidemic swept nation, 1957; commercial jet air service began, 1958; farm population in U.S. declined, 1958; computer chip patented by American scientists, 1959; synthetic penicillin developed, 1959; compact cars became more popular, 1959

# Winsome Murmurs from the 1950s

*"Who are these DARs I keep hearing about?" inquired one LaGrange teenager of another. "I don't exactly know," her friend replied, "but I believe they were the WACs of the Revolutionary War."*

*He gazed admiringly at the chorine's costume. "Who made her dress?" he asked his companion. "I'm not sure," was the reply, "but I imagine it was the police."*

*A father was lecturing his 10-year-old son about his poor report card. The lad listened patiently until a break in the monologue gave him a chance to ask his father, "What do you think my trouble is—heredity or environment?"*

*This year there are motorcars for the young-at-heart, for leaders in the world of affairs, for the man who demands the finest and for those who look beyond tomorrow. Are there cars for the people who just want to get to work and back?*

*Wives who love the truth are much happier if they don't ask too many questions.*

*A local lawyer in Superior Court yesterday had a novel, if not convincing, reason why his client was down at the still when the revenuers arrived. He was down there "hunting muscadines to feed his poor old Pa," the lawyer told the jury. The jury didn't believe him. The fellow got one to two years.*

*Mrs. Ben Thompson entertained at a hobo-style party on Saturday afternoon at the Coca-Cola Hall in LaGrange, honoring her son, Benjy, on his eighth birthday. Young guests, dressed like hoboes, enjoyed games, after which, sitting on newspapers, they gathered around a make-believe fire for singing and story-telling.*

*Eleanor's Letter—A man arrested for stealing a car recently told our police reporter that he found the car standing in front of a cemetery and thought the owner was dead.*

*Eleanor's Letter—The folks who live in the Broad Street Apartments are always amazed when Jack Davis drives his T-Model Ford out of the garage; amazed that a motor car, as old as that one, will still run. It must be at least 24 years old. Keeping the motor primed, and whatever else you do to motors, is one of Jack's hobbies. It's a rare treat for the youngsters in LaGrange to take a ride with Jack in his car.*

*A 17-year-old LaGrange boy, who had been involved in two accidents within a month, got a suspended sentence today on the promise he will attend church and Sunday School for the next twelve months. The boy's pastor appeared in his behalf and told the city recorder the boy was a churchgoer and ordinarily not careless. The boy promised to drive more carefully and to go to church regularly. His driver's license was suspended for 60 days, and a suspended fine of $25 hangs over him if he has another accident anytime soon.*

*Forgetting the past, instead of using it for the future, will keep you from getting any place in the present.*

CHAPTER 8
# The 1960s

From *LaGrange Daily News*

The 1960s decade, and specifically the year 1960, brought many promises of more progress to come. So much was happening on the national scene, as well as locally, that brought changes in the lives of LaGrange and Troup County residents.

LaGrange felt its importance early in the decade when, on October 10, 1960, the Democratic presidential candidate, Senator John F. Kennedy, came by LaGrange while he was on what a LaGrange *Daily News* reporter called "a whirlwind visit to Georgia" before he was elected to office in November of that year.

Earlier that October day, Senator Kennedy had scheduled speeches in Columbus and Warm Springs, where he had addressed a crowd from the steps of the Little White House in the tradition of the war-time president Franklin D. Roosevelt. After his remarks there, the *Daily News* reported that "a motorcade brought him to the LaGrange-Callaway Airport."

People had lined the streets in LaGrange, leading to the airport, to catch a glimpse of the first presidential candidate to visit here in many years. Local school authorities had dismissed classes for his visit, so schoolchildren and LaGrange College students were among those waiting to see him. The *Daily News* account of his visit offers us a good description of the excitement of the crowd, as follows: "His arrival brought applause from the men and sometimes screams of delight from the women. The youthful Senator's appeal to the women in the crowd was evident from the time his motorcade came into view. Squeals like those that roc' n' roll singers draw rang out."

After brief remarks at the airport, where an estimated crowd of three thousand people waited to see him, he boarded his private plane, the Caroline, and took off for another appearance in Columbia, South Carolina.

An editorial in the local daily that followed the Kennedy visit posed this question: "Two-Party System Over Horizon?" and closed with the following observations:

> *Personal visits by a presidential candidate always swing a certain amount of votes, no matter what issues are involved. To offset the dent which Kennedy made possible in his West Georgia swing, a major campaign appearance by vice-presidential candidate, Henry Cabot Lodge, may be forthcoming. Newnan Republicans have invited the former United Nations Ambassador to a barbecue in Newnan. Plans call for him to land and take off from Callaway Airport in LaGrange. Thus the presidential campaign continues. Georgia may not be too far away from a two-party system.*

Kennedy's brief visit brought big dividends here and in the county, as the published, after-the-election results showed that Troup County endorsed Kennedy and other Democratic candidates by 67 percent.

An editorial in the *Daily News* in June 1960 marked the early action on a proposed, destined-for-success dam for the Chattahoochee River that would have far-reaching effects on the entire area of the Southeast. The editorial read almost like a front-page news story, as it announced that "federal engineers, now surveying an area in Troup County for a proposed multi-purpose dam across the Chattahoochee River, expect to make a report in September."

The writer went on to say, "The survey is two-thirds complete, following investigations of the dam site's flood damage, stream flow and spillway or reservoir area. Still incomplete are reports on the plans and estimated cost of any structures, relocations of roads and railroads and core sampling." The editorial concluded with this statement: "As soon as the study is made public, Troup County citizens can get the experts' viewpoint on the prospects for the dam."

By 1961, the U.S. Army Corps of Engineers had recommended construction of the multipurpose dam on the Chattahoochee River near West Point, according to continuing news reports in the *Daily News*. The dam project received congressional approval in October 1962, bringing an enthusiastic response from citizens and leaders in the city and county.

Patience started paying off in this case; on November 15, 1963, the *Daily News* reported that "a House Committee has approved $350,000 in planning funds for the dam project, as requested in the U.S. Corps of Engineers report."

After periodic updates on the necessary clearing and different phases of construction in the ensuing years, in December 1969, the *Daily News* reported that "the concrete work on the West Point Reservoir Dam is 87 percent complete."

The overall completion of the West Point Dam will be reported in the upcoming chapter on the decade of the 1970s.

In LaGrange homes during the 1960s, space exploration was a favorite topic. At that time, spaceships were not just being seen in comic strips. Even belief in "flying saucers" had become more plausible, because reports of sightings were often appearing in the news columns of the local newspaper.

An editorial in the *Daily News* in April 1960 mentioned "flying saucers" in a credible way, reporting that the United States Air Force, in a recent directive, had issued a warning to its command "to treat sightings of unidentified objects as serious business."

For months there had been a cloak of secrecy surrounding the official attitude toward the saucers. Many of those reported sightings, after investigations, had turned out to be U.S. weather balloons or high-flying airships reflecting the sun's rays. The editorial concluded with this statement: "Now, the public might be in a better position to evaluate future sightings."

An even more intriguing development came in August 1960, when a news story was published in the *Daily News* revealing the secret that our own country was considering launching a "flying saucer" for inner space. In part, it read:

> *The Defense Department, which insists there are no "flying saucers" bringing little men from outer space, has disclosed a photo of a saucer it is developing to haul big men in inner space. The picture showed a pie-shaped craft with a fan-like apparatus running through the center and two plastic canopies on top. The photo was the first official picture ever released of this country's planned "flying saucer." Little is ever said in Washington about the hush-hush project. But it is known that the United States is pushing development of the radical new aircraft, which the Soviets also are assumed to be working on. Reliable military sources said the saucer would provide a modern airborne cavalry "the likes of which have never been seen in*

*warfare." Avro Aircraft of Canada, which is developing the saucer for the United States, said last October, the strange vehicle made a successful flight inside a hangar, rising on a cushion of air jetted from beneath the craft.*

Later research reported that this project was cancelled in 1961 when the design proved too unstable.

In December 1961, the *Daily News* reported, "The Citizens and Southern National Bank has chosen LaGrange as the site for a 54,000-cubic-foot underground vault, designed to protect key records of individuals and businesses, and it will be constructed on a site bounded by Broad, Trinity and Vernon streets. The vast underground vault will be named 'Fort Georgia.'" The report added that the services of the vault would be available to individuals, businesses, municipalities and other governmental offices. Construction was to begin as soon as specifications were completed. Further information revealed: "LaGrange was selected as the site for the vault after consultation with Civil Defense officials because it is believed that LaGrange would encounter less fallout than other areas in Georgia in case of a nuclear attack."

For a few weeks in December 1961 and early January 1962, headlines in the *Daily News* were reporting on a visit to LaGrange by a gypsy queen and her faithful band of followers. Sue Newsom in her "Here and There" column revealed that the queen had been recuperating in an Alabama hospital following a heart attack. En route to Atlanta for further treatment, she became too ill to travel farther and stopped at the City-County Hospital in LaGrange. Sue added these details: "There is a tribal law of some kind that the 'flock' stays with the Queen. We understand that the band has camped in the parking lot of the hospital. The Queen seems to have passed the crisis, but will have to remain hospitalized here about three more weeks."

This was just the beginning of the captivating saga. A later write-up reported that after the word of their queen's illness had spread through gypsy colonies, "she attracted a horde of gypsies to LaGrange, but they did not come in the traditional horse-drawn carts." "As many as 150 gypsies," according to Hospital Administrator Joe Taylor, "came in automobiles, some of them in late model Cadillacs."

The *Daily News* continued to report the band members' "creating problems for hospital personnel. Gypsies have been sleeping in the chapel and on conference room tables in the hospital. Other times they lounge around on the sofas in the waiting rooms. Another time, the man claiming to be the King of the band, used one of the patient bathrooms to take a shower."

"Many strange stories were circulated about their actions while in LaGrange," according to the *Daily News*. The most frightening was probably a report that a number of the gypsies showed up in a hospital corridor with candles they intended to light in the queen's room. Had they succeeded in their plan, it could have brought devastating results, since she was in an oxygen tent at the time. Fortunately, they were stopped by a doctor.

The *Daily News* reported, "On the afternoon of January 15, the Queen and her band of followers left LaGrange, having been warned by City-County Hospital officials that she was in no condition to be moved." They left behind a hospital bill and were extremely secretive about their destination. At that time they didn't even give it to the ambulance driver who came for the queen. Later he reported he took her to a hotel in Atlanta.

In a front-page story by Miss Eleanor Orr, *Daily News* staff writer, announcing the queen's departure, she wrote:

> *The Gypsy Queen has gone. Rarely has a visitor in LaGrange occasioned more conversation than the dusky, luminous-eyed Queen who was brought to City-County Hospital on December 2, with what hospital authorities termed "serious heart and kidney ailments." As the days passed, the gypsy band with her dwindled until there were only about seven who were constant in their vigil. They included the Queen's husband, who claimed to be the King of the band; her sister with her husband, who disputed the husband's claim of kingship; and four children, believed to be the Queen's. "Miss Sally," as the hospital nurses called the Queen, became a favorite for she was amenable. It was her followers who posed the problems.*

The *Daily News* covered all the exploration in outer space that was often occurring in the decade of the 1960s and even earlier.

LaGrange residents had shared the disappointment of all Americans when the Soviets launched Sputnik, the first man-made shuttle in the late 1950s, and when Yuri Gagarin, the Soviet cosmonaut, became the first man to orbit the earth in a space flight in 1961.

But these accomplishments by the Russians did not lessen the pride of our nation and LaGrange readers later in 1961, when the news reports announced that Alan Shepard Jr. had become the first American in space, or when John Glenn was the first American to orbit the earth in 1962.

We will leave the continuing space coverage for a short while to report on what was being termed by news reports as "a possible World War III threat"—the Cuban missile crisis in 1962.

In early October 1962, LaGrange residents, as well as other Americans, were reading disturbing news in local newspapers. The *Daily News* at that time reported, "Castro admits there are Red military technicians in Cuba."

The news item appeared on the back page of the *Daily News*, but not many days had passed before news about the "Soviet presence in Cuba" was taking front-page space regularly—in fact, almost every day.

By mid-October, President John F. Kennedy had met with Russia's Gromyko for what was reported in the *News* to have been "a 'Cold War' discussion, before a planned talk to be held later between Kennedy and Khrushchev in the United States. Our national officials say Kennedy will undoubtedly touch on the continued Soviet build-up in Cuba when the two leaders meet."

The threat of confrontation with the Soviets about Cuba became more serious when, on October 23, a front-page headline reported, "Soviet Ships Head Toward Explosive Test with U.S." The story added: "U.S. planes and ships have been dispersed to start a blockade against Soviet shipments of aggressive weapons to the Communist-dominated island."

The Cuban missile crisis dominated the news in the remaining October issues of the *Daily News*. Each day, front-page reminders of the situation in Cuba continued as a confrontation was developing.

A frightening news report was published in the *Daily News* on October 24 stating that "government sources said plans were going forward for a full-scale invasion of Cuba, if present U.S. measures prove inadequate to neutralize the island as a 'threat to the United States.'"

The increasing international unrest brought "United Nations talks between U.S. Ambassador Adlai Stevenson and Soviet Foreign Minister Zorin," according to the *Daily News*. On October 27, Khrushchev offered "to withdraw the offensive forces in Cuba if the United States would withdraw 'similar weapons' from Turkey."

President Kennedy "stood tall" throughout the crisis, and an editorial in the October 27 issue of the *Daily News* expressed his decision. The editorial was entitled "Peace of World Hanging by Very Slender Thread," and it included a quote from Kennedy that said, in part: "United States Policy will be to regard any nuclear missile launched from Cuba against any nation in the Western Hemisphere as an attack by Russia on the United States, requiring full retaliation against the Soviet Union."

Because Fort Benning, in Columbus, was considered to be a possible target for bombing in case of an enemy air attack, and because of LaGrange's proximity to Columbus, local authorities and civil defense representatives believed that our specific location was vulnerable to an attack, should one come. Plans were made to provide fallout shelters to be used in LaGrange in the event of an emergency, according to frequent updates in the *Daily News*. Local merchants reported increased buying of emergency items and supplies, like flashlights, water and food items, for home shelters set up during this time.

A community underground fallout shelter was set up near the First United Methodist Church in LaGrange. "Civil Defense representatives identified three shelters to be used by LaGrange College students and Registered Nurses were assigned to each shelter," according to *Daily News* reports. "Local school buildings were rejected as shelters because school board authorities felt that students 'would be as safe at home as they would be at school in case of a nuclear attack.'"

The Cuban situation seemed to be somewhat better for a short while after United Nations acting secretary-general Thant made an official visit to Cuba in an effort to ease the tension, but United States surveillance of

The First Methodist Church, built in 1898. It was replaced by a new sanctuary at the same site in 1964. It is believed to be the oldest Troup County institution on its original site.

the sea lanes in and out of Cuba continued, with the U.S. Navy inspecting Russian freighters. Because of the continuing concern of its readers, the *Daily News* reported all of these developments in Cuba on a daily basis.

Finally, on November 10, the newspaper reported that "42 missiles had been removed from Cuba, the number the Russians claimed to have sent." By November 20, "The Cuban blockade was ordered lifted," according to the *News*, and the Russians had agreed to remove Russian jet bombers from Cuba. The presence of the bombers had been another point of contention to the United States.

In 1963, a local landmark for almost sixty-five years, the LaGrange First Methodist Church building, was razed in order to have a larger sanctuary, as reported in the *Daily News*. Some of the materials from the beloved structure, including Belgian stained-glass windows, were used later in the decade in constructing the LaGrange College Chapel.

On November 22, 1963, LaGrange and the entire nation were in shock at the heartbreaking news that our president, John F. Kennedy, had been "killed in Texas."

In a banner headline and story, the *Daily News* reported, "President John Fitzgerald Kennedy was shot to death by an assassin, as he rode through downtown Dallas in an open car with Texas Governor John B. Connally. The president was shot once in the head. Connally was gravely wounded." The story added that Mrs. Kennedy and Mrs. Connally were in the car with their husbands and that Vice President Lyndon Johnson was in a car behind the president.

The following day, the *News* brought more details of the events that followed the assassination—"the swearing in of the vice president, Lyndon Johnson, on board Air Force One prior to its return to Washington," and "the arrest of Lee Harvey Oswald, identified as chairman of a 'Fair Play for Cuba Committee.'"

Oswald was charged with the murders of the president and a Dallas policeman, J.D. Tippitt, thirty-nine, shot in the line of duty, according to a follow-up story in the newspaper. Oswald was later identified as an "avowed Marxist and Fidel Castro supporter, who denied any knowledge of the assassination when he was arrested."

A front-page editorial in the *Daily News* emphasized the importance of the writer's feelings about the assassination and loss of our nation's president when he wrote:

*The assassination of the President of the United States is inconceivable in our time of enlightened intelligence. It will remain for history to write the final chapter to the atrocious act. As the news erupted spontaneously across the nation, we at first refused to believe. Then, we were devastated by the horrible truth. Today we stand in silence and sorrow for the murder of a man who becomes a martyr to his beliefs. This is not a sorrow that belongs to a few; it is a sorrow that belongs to an entire nation. This is time for us to stop to pray...for we have felt the impact of the sniper's bullet.*

On November 25, the day of the funeral, a headline in the local newspaper read "LaGrange Halts in Tribute to Late President," followed by a story describing what happened locally. "Everything stopped," the news writer reported, "doors to schools, businesses, banks, institutions and government agencies were all closed in memoriam to the late John F. Kennedy. Doors to all the churches in LaGrange and in the county were open for prayer and memorial services, planned by their congregations."

On Saturday night, November 23, LaGrange College held a memorial service attended by old and young people from town, as well as college faculty and students, filling the Dobbs Auditorium on the Hill. At that service, college president Waights G. Henry Jr. said: "Out of the sorrow of this occasion, society will become more of a cohesive force, and the president's death will bring about greater mutual understanding, a renewed spirit of brotherhood and even world peace."

This edition of the newspaper also confirmed the incredible news that "Oswald had been shot and killed by a self-appointed executioner before a nationwide television audience." Further details in the report "identified the killer as Jack Ruby, a one-time Chicago street brawler and owner of a Dallas night club, who fired one shot and killed Oswald, as authorities were preparing to take him to a maximum security cell at the county jail in Dallas." Ruby had told the arresting officers that he decided "to obviate the legal processes of a trial by executing Oswald himself," according to the news report.

Ruby's story was never fully believed by Dallas police authorities or the district attorney there. On November 30, the nation's new president, Lyndon Johnson, appointed a seven-member commission to probe the slaying of President Kennedy, according to the *Daily News*.

Two more assassinations that "rocked" the nation came later in the decade of the 1960s, with the murders of Martin Luther King Jr., the civil rights leader, in Memphis, Tennessee, in 1968; and Robert F. Kennedy, a presidential candidate and brother of the late president John F. Kennedy, who was shot in California, also in 1968. Both national tragedies were reported at length in the *Daily News*.

Foreseeing the coming mandate to integrate the schools in LaGrange and in the county, school authorities made the decision to integrate LaGrange High School and Troup High School in 1965. This was done under the "Freedom of Choice" plan. The transition went smoothly, according to *Daily News* reports. Further integration of the local and county school systems will be reported in the decade of the 1970s.

In 1965, American troops began fighting in the Vietnam War. LaGrange and Troup County had many servicemen and -women in the armed forces, many serving in the war zone. Service awards and promotions were announced in many issues of the *Daily News*. Red Cross volunteers in LaGrange and all of Troup County supported the troops with Christmas packages and other remembrances.

There will be a deficiency in the number of reports on the Vietnam War in this chronicle, compared to the coverage of other wars, and some other important local events are not covered in depth, because the years 1964 through 1968 were not in the years researched month by month for the "Memoried Glances" column.

Reports on the progress of the war published in the *Daily News* were standard wire service reports. It must be noted, however, that many fine young American men and women, including many from LaGrange and Troup County, served our nation bravely and effectively in the armed forces all during this time. Some lost their lives, and many were prisoners of war. The *Daily News* was faithful in reporting the war news, always keeping local residents informed about our area's men and women in the service.

The first soldier from LaGrange to die in Vietnam was Grady Keith Embrey, a private first class in the United States Army's Airborne Brigade. He was nineteen on September 19, 1965, when he was killed in Vietnam while on a "search and destroy" mission, according to a report published in *For Love of Country*, a well-researched compilation of Troup County veterans who died in service from 1900 to 2000, by John Thomas West, MD. The news of Embrey's death, and the return of his body to LaGrange on September 28, 1965, also appeared in the *Daily News*. A funeral was held in the Ida Cason Callaway Chapel at the First Baptist Church in LaGrange, and full military burial service followed at Shadowlawn Cemetery. Private

First Class Embrey had a brother, Terry Embrey, a seaman apprentice on submarine duty stationed at New London, Connecticut.

On February 7, 1966, a navy pilot from LaGrange, Commander Render Crayton, was captured by the North Vietnamese and was a prisoner of war for the next seven years, according to a report in the *Daily News*. A full report of his release and return to the States is included in the decade of the 1970s, after the Vietnam cease fire was reported when our nation's leaders withdrew our ground troops from Vietnam.

Just as the Cuban missile crisis had dominated the news in October 1962 and President Kennedy's assassination had in late 1963, space flights and news of the space program dominated the pages of the *Daily News* in the remaining years of the 1960s.

Everyone in LaGrange shared the grief of all Americans when we read of the first space test disaster at Cape Kennedy in 1967. NASA's perseverance and expertise brought "Apollo 8 astronauts' successful blast into orbit around the moon in 1968," according to the *Daily News*.

Space exploration was advanced by all the Apollo flights in 1969, all leading up to Apollo 11's flight, when Neil Armstrong became the first person to set foot on the moon in July 1969. On July 21, the *Daily News* published this report: "Man Walks on Moon—America's two moon pioneers completed man's first exploit of the lunar surface today. Neil A. Armstrong and Edwin E. Aldrin are the first humans to set foot on the lunar surface. Michael Collins circled the moon in the Apollo 11 command ship for their return to earth."

In August 1969, the *Daily News* reported that the moon rocks the space pioneers had brought home with them were much older than first expected. The story added, "According to the scientists who have examined the Apollo 11 moon rocks, the rocks date back 'billions of years' and perhaps even to the birth of the solar system. The chief scientist at the Houston Space Center says that the moon rocks are at least as old as the most ancient rocks found in the earth's crust, which date back about 3.3 billion years."

This brief account in the *Daily News* of a November 1969 space flight read: "Apollo 12 Thunders Off Amid Jolting Lightning—America's three-man Apollo 12 crew successfully blasted off on a second moon-landing mission despite a last minute thunderstorm that may have jolted the booster rocket with a lightning bolt." This turned out to be another successful flight in spite of the bad weather on blast-off. After an on-target landing on the moon, Apollo 12 returned to earth safely with samples of lunar soil, as reported in the local daily. Pete Conrad was flight commander.

The final coverage of the space program reported in this decade was about space prayers made by American astronauts. In a story in the *Daily News* in December 1969, this appeared:

> *Court Dismisses Suit Asking Space Prayer Ban—A federal judge in Austin, Texas dismissed Madalyn Murray O'Hair's suit seeking to ban the broadcast of space prayers by American astronauts. U.S. District Judge Jack Roberts said a decision in favor of Mrs. O'Hair, an Austin atheist and housewife, would have violated the religious rights of astronauts. "The First Amendment does not require the states to be hostile to religion, but only neutral," Roberts said in his opinion.*

Closing this decade on a local note with what seemed to be the "sport of the decade" for LaGrange and Troup County high school teams and fans, it is important to note that sports items in the *Daily News* reported, "LaGrange High School won the state basketball AAA championship in 1963, and again in 1965. Troup High School won its second consecutive regional AA basketball championship in 1969." Many winning games and tournaments, as well as the outstanding players and coaches on both teams, were often featured on the *Daily News*'s sports pages throughout the basketball seasons in the '60s.

## Mosaic Musings from the 1960s

*Even the goal posts at Callaway Stadium are dressed up for Christmas. It seems some paper streamers the students used to decorate them were left on and the rain faded them and now they are pink.*

*We heard recently about a parent who thought it wise to levy a withholding tax on his child's allowance in order that he might become hardened to paying a tax while he was young. This parent might have something, but we would be in favor of shielding the younger generation as long as possible because his future is sure to be a bleak one as far as taxes are concerned.*

*In an election year, politicians who find fault with everything proposed by the opposition ought to have their motives examined. Voters who believe everything the politicians say ought to have their heads examined.*

*We cannot qualify as an expert or even a near expert on international matters. But, this we believe: There is absolutely no advantage for this country in continuing the pussy-footing policy that has been in effect toward "Communist Castro." We may win by a hard attitude. We will certainly not win by being softies.*

## OPENINGS/FOUNDINGS

New post office building, 1962; new First United Methodist Church sanctuary, 1964; new chapel at LaGrange College, 1965; Troup County Area Vocational Technical School, 1966; new LaGrange water pollution plant, 1966; Callaway Foundation Inc. established forty Fuller E. Callaway professional chairs at Georgia colleges and universities, 1968; establishment of Sims Nursing Scholarships by Fuller E. Callaway Foundation, 1967

## ORGANIZATIONS

Chattahoochee Valley Art Association, 1963

## HAPPENINGS

Devastating flood in West Point, 1961; Harwell Avenue School burned in LaGrange, 1963; first local sidewalk art show, 1963; merger of West Point Manufacturing Company and Pepperell, Inc., 1965; Troup High School and LaGrange High School integrated under "Freedom of Choice" plan, 1965; LaGrange High School State AAA basketball champions, 1963 and 1965; groundbreaking for construction of West Point Dam, 1966; LaGrange College initiated night classes, 1967; new clubhouse built for Highland Country Club, 1967; Callaway Mills sold to Deering-Milliken & Company (this brought a close to home-owned textile mills at that time), 1968; plans announced for industrial park for LaGrange by chamber of commerce and Callaway Foundation Inc., 1969; Troup County High School Regional AA basketball champions for second consecutive year, 1969; many military awards presented to LaGrange and Troup County men and women for military service in Vietnam, 1965–69

Highland Country Club's clubhouse, built in 1923. It was razed and replaced with a new building at the same site in 1967.

## 1960s DECADE REVIEW—NATIONALLY

Civil rights movement began in Greensboro, North Carolina, 1960; Peace Corps established, 1961; Cuban missile crisis, 1962; President Kennedy assassinated, 1963; Lyndon B. Johnson sworn in as president, 1963; civil rights march in Washington, 1963; inauguration of women's rights movement, 1963; Civil Rights Act passed by Congress outlawing segregation, 1964; U.S. surgeon general issued health warnings about smoking, 1964; U.S. troops in Vietnam War, 1965; Medicare launched in United States, 1966; first heart transplant surgery successful (patient died eighteen days later of double pneumonia), 1967; Martin Luther King Jr., civil rights leader, assassinated, 1968; Robert F. Kennedy, presidential candidate, assassinated, 1968; Richard M. Nixon sworn in as thirty-seventh president of the United States, 1969; Apollo 11's Neil Armstrong, first person to set foot on the moon, 1969

# WINSOME MURMURS FROM THE 1960S

*It is predicted that business is to be so good in 1960 that a business can work itself into a nervous breakdown.*

*It's hard to explain to a child why a nation that is spending billions of dollars on A-bombs is trying to outlaw firecrackers.*

*Some of the Democratic presidential hopefuls have not yet announced their candidacies. They are too out of breath from running.*

*They call it "giving the bride away" but dad's checkbook shows it cost him a pretty penny to close the deal.*

*A local firm says, "We have the best terms in town—one hundred percent down and nothing a week."*

*Eleanor's Letter—An "old timer," said Chattahoochee Charlie, "is one who remembers when 'on time' meant being punctual rather than an accepted way of making a purchase."*

*Taxes are staggering, but they never go down.*

*Here and There: Sweet young thing to loving beau who has just proposed to her. "Of course I could live on what you make…But what would you live on?"*

*Here and There: A man went to the psychiatrist and told him he wanted help because he thought he was a dog. When the psychiatrist asked him how long he had been thinking he was a dog, he replied, "Ever since I was a puppy."*

CHAPTER 9

# The 1970s

## *The Decade of the Bicentennial*

From *LaGrange Daily News*

This was an especially significant decade to citizens of LaGrange because of local preparations that began early for the observance of our nation's bicentennial in 1976. The year 1970, however, began in LaGrange with news that ranged from the inevitable to the inane, both extremes coming in news from our public schools.

The inevitable and significant news was announced in the *Daily News* in January 1970 with the headlines, "Complete Integration Set Here September 1." This followed the United States Supreme Court's order for "the complete integration of fourteen Dixie school districts to integrate by February 1, including three Georgia school districts in Bibb, Burke and Houston counties."

LaGrange and Troup County school systems were already working on plans for integrating the schools here; in fact, the 1954 ruling of the Supreme Court, stating that "no child should be barred from any school because of nationality, race or creed," had come as a warning that something must be done. In the mid-'60s, there had been a minimum of integration in local public schools, but this 1970 announcement brought the necessity for a formal policy.

The 1970–71 school year's beginning in September marked the official integration of the LaGrange and Troup County public schools. This time, as in the earlier integration of the high schools in the '60s, the transition was a smooth one.

Some anonymous person once said, "A little nonsense now and then is relished by the wisest men."

The inane and trivial news came in the *Daily News* in April 1970 with the headline "Hemline Battle at Troup High School." Two students had "protested the new dress and grooming code at Troup High, requiring that hemlines be not more than eight inches above the knee."

The two girls had arrived at school wearing mini-dresses; teachers had measured the skirts and found that they violated the rule. The girls were sent home to change their clothes. The news report explained that "they returned to school wearing mid-calf length dresses." The girls protested the ruling, but "the code was not changed," according to a later report in the *News*.

The dress and grooming code came up again at Troup High in December of that same year. Three boys had appealed the school's hair ruling, bringing another review of the code. This was followed by the headline in the *Daily News* "Troup Okays Pant Suits, Retains 8-Inch Skirt Rule."

The news story explained that the Troup County Board of Education had reconsidered the rules and amended the dress and grooming code by allowing girls to wear pants to class. "The board confirmed their 'eight-inches the knee,' as the maximum allowed for skirts. They did not change their grooming policy, 'hair cannot be worn over the collar, ears or eyebrows.'"

A similar question came up later in that year at LaGrange High School. The *Daily News* reported, "A review and updating of the code of dress and grooming for LHS students was recommended to the City Board of Education, by a special committee of students, parents and teachers, appointed at the request of Principal Neil Sherrod." The suggested code stated, "It will be up to parents to decide if their daughter's dress is too short, or their son's hair too long."

In the summer and early fall of 1970, folks in Hogansville were making plans to celebrate the town's centennial on October 12. The *Daily News* reported, "Hogansville townspeople are collecting old-fashioned items used in the 1870s." The men there were growing beards, and the ladies were looking for bonnets and making long dresses for costumes appropriate for that period in history. Plans called for "a week-long celebration, October 12–18."

An important occurrence in LaGrange in 1971 came when James S. Duncan became the first black man in the history of the city to be named to the local school board. He served as a member from 1971 to 1987 and as chairman in 1975 and 1976.

In the first two years of the 1970s, thoughts of LaGrange residents were often turning to American history and to the nation's bicentennial and its celebration to come later in the decade.

When LaGrange College president Dr. Waights G. Henry Jr. was on a trip abroad in the summer of 1972, he visited in France, where he was given a special American flag, one that, according to the *Daily News*, "had flown 24-hours-a-day over the grave of the Marquis de Lafayette." The story explained, "By tradition, each year, a flag was lowered annually on Independence Day and given to an institution or an individual who had some contact with Lafayette, or who had helped improve relations with France."

Dr. Henry's well-known interest in the Revolutionary War hero Lafayette and the French connection, with LaGrange having been named for the estate of the Marquis, made Dr. Henry an appropriate person to receive the special flag.

There will be more about Dr. Henry and his involvement with the LaGrange Bicentennial Commission, as its chairman, later in this decade.

Although advance planning for the bicentennial celebration seemed to take precedence over other news in the *Daily News* during the years leading up to its 1976 observance, another project, of primary interest to local citizens and spanning two decades, was the West Point Dam across the Chattahoochee River. These two topics will often seem to "take turns" in our chronicle as developments in both projects occurred. The dam was mentioned earlier in the 1960s decade chapter.

That earlier reference had come in December 1969, when it was projected in a *Daily News* story that "the dam project will require an expenditure of $64.2 million and is expected to be completed in June of 1970."

How the authorities wished this could have been true! Much more time and more increases in cost were to come before the dam would become a reality, but there would be good news along the way, despite the delays in the dam's completion.

An important development in the dam project was reported in the *Daily News* in December 1970, when the announcement was made, "Bids are being taken for the construction of the powerhouse facility at the West Point Dam." At that time it was expected "to require three-and-a-half years to build the powerhouse and the appurtenance works, at a cost in excess of $10 million. Completion of the overall project was programmed for completion in 1974."

In November 1972, James E. Morgan, real estate manager for the West Point Dam project, told LaGrange Rotarians, as reported in the *Daily News*, "You can expect to fish in the waters of the lake by June of 1974." He predicted "the project's completion by September of 1974."

That same month, in 1972, the newspaper reported a celebration going on in another part of the world that offered some amusing observations:

> *As Queen Elizabeth and Prince Phillip celebrate their silver wedding anniversary in England, Britons are beginning to wonder whether the monarchy is as relevant as it once was. Some of the older generation members claim that in an age of anarchy, monarchy is even more valid as a unifying force in British society. Others, more pessimistic, doubt whether the monarchy will last more than this century and predict that Prince Charles, now 24, will be the last British sovereign. If the public thinks about Charles at all, it is as an earnest, plodding young man, a bit on the dull side.*

In December 1972, the *Daily News* printed an important notice for LaGrange parents of small children about an appearance to be made by Santa Claus as he came through our town on board a regularly scheduled passenger train. The notice read:

> *Santa's sleigh has broken down and the reindeer can only fly in snowy weather, so 'ol Saint Nick will make a brief stop in LaGrange by train on Saturday morning about 10 o'clock. Santa will stop in front of the freight office on Morgan Street in LaGrange. He will have treats to give the children who come to see him engineering the train.*

Long-awaited news on January 27, 1973, brought the following headline: "Vietnam Fighting Ends at 7 P.M." The report continued: "LaGrange will hold ceremonies on the Square to celebrate the end of hostilities and to honor the men who gave their lives in the Vietnam War, as well as all those who served in the 12-year conflict in Southeast Asia. The cease-fire also brings notice of the release, within 60 days, of all Prisoners of War."

A navy pilot from LaGrange, Commander Render Crayton, had been reported as captured by the enemy in February 1966 after being shot down while on a strike mission over North Vietnam, as reported in the *Daily News* in the '60s. During the intervening years, while he was in prison, his mother, Mrs. Mary Jane Crayton of LaGrange, as reported in the *Daily News* at that time, "made a trip to Paris and Geneva with the National League of Families of Prisoners to make an appeal for the release of all Vietnam POWs."

In February 1973, the *Daily News* reported, "Commander Render Crayton was among the first Prisoners of War to be released by the Communists; in fact, he was aboard the first plane to land at Clark Air Force Base in the Philippines."

The big celebration for his return was not held in LaGrange until May 1973, when the newspaper estimated that "2,500 people weathered the rain and wind to come out to hear from Commander Crayton on his return to LaGrange after his seven years as a POW in a North Vietnamese prison."

The newspaper reported, "The event was a combination 'Welcome Home Ceremony and Lions Club Flag Dedication,' held on Armed Forces Day." At the same event, a "Street of Flags," a project of the LaGrange Lions Club, was "dedicated to the community to be used on special occasions, as a reminder of patriotism and the American way of life." The local Lions Club had purchased 135 all-weather flags, and the City of LaGrange cooperated with the effort by attaching many of the flags to parking meters around the square. Other groups sponsoring the project included the Recruiting Service of LaGrange and the *LaGrange Daily News*.

More about Captain Render Crayton, who had been promoted and stationed in California, came in the *News* in January 1975, when he was "to receive seven military awards in Navy ceremonies at the Naval Air Station in San Diego—the Distinguished Service Medal, two Silver Stars and four Bronze Stars, earned for his service in the Vietnam War."

In January 1974, the *Daily News* reported, "The West Point Dam project, which is 80 percent complete, has been credited with averting $50,000 in flood damages after heavy rains over Georgia during the last weekend in December."

This was the first time the dam had been able to prevent flooding, according to the statement from government officials published in the *Daily News*. "Without the dam," a spokesman said, "the river would have peaked at 21 feet; flood stage in West Point is 19 feet."

Formal plans for the local celebration of the bicentennial were continuing during this time in the 1970s. In April 1974, a new development was announced in the *Daily News* when Dr. Waights G. Henry Jr., president of

LaGrange College and Bicentennial Commission chairman, addressed a group of merchants and property owners from the Court Square area at a luncheon meeting.

Dr. Henry proposed that an Italian-cast statue of the Marquis de Lafayette be erected on a pedestal in the center of the city's fountain on the Square. The work, by an American sculptor, was at that time being shipped to America from France, made possible by a grant from Callaway Foundation, Inc.

"The original plan," Dr. Henry explained, "was to place the statue on the LaGrange College campus. After consideration by College and Foundation officials," the newspaper account added, "they felt it was more appropriate to place the statue in a prominent location in downtown LaGrange because of the honor founders of our city had given the Revolutionary War hero in naming the city for his estate in France."

This proposal was approved by the city, as confirmed in the *Daily News* in May 1974, when the LaGrange City Council "announced it had received a grant from Callaway Foundation, Inc. to pay the cost of erecting the statue of Lafayette on the Square." Further actions regarding the statue were reported in news items in September 1974; the first was when the LaGrange City Council passed an ordinance "renaming Court Square, 'Lafayette Square,' in memory of the Marquis," the change to become effective on November

Lafayette Square as it appears today, on the site of the old Troup County Courthouse. *Bill Holt, photographer.*

1. It was also announced at that time that "the council had approved an agreement with LaGrange College to be responsible for protecting and maintaining the statue, on permanent loan to the city of LaGrange, while it is located on the Square."

The other September news relating to the statue of Lafayette brought an announcement:

> *On September 19, the newly organized LaGrange Junior Service League will sell Bicentennial Medals through the LaGrange Bicentennial Commission, at the Citizens and Southern National Bank, in conjunction with the first unveiling of the statue, which will remain on temporary display at the bank, until its placement on the Square. Proceeds from the sale of the medals will be used to sponsor locally-planned events for the 200$^{th}$ anniversary of the United States.*

"The statue of the Marquis de Lafayette took one giant step on New Year's Day, 1975," the *Daily News* reported, "from the lobby of the Citizens and Southern Bank on Main Street to its permanent home on a pedestal in Memorial Park." Its move up Main Street, from the bank to the square, was observed by many local citizens who watched the positioning of the new guardian of the square with interest. Once again, history was made in LaGrange that day. More information followed:

> *The statue is a reproduction of a statue located in LePuy, France, where Lafayette's estate was located. The original statue was confiscated by the Germans in World War II, but was stolen back by the French and buried. Following the war it was dug up and returned to its place of honor in LePuy. Dedication ceremonies for the statue will take place on February 21, 1976.*

During the remaining months of 1975, before another important area dedication, the West Point Dam made the news almost every month, beginning with a report from the General Accounting Office in Washington that was published in the *Daily News* in March. The story reported, "The cost overrun on the West Point Dam amounted to 112 percent." It also reminded readers that "the original estimated cost, when it started in 1965, was $53 million, revised to $64.2 million in 1969."

In May, the *Daily News* announced, "The gates on the West Point Dam are closed, and the lake is beginning to fill." The lake was expected to reach its summer peak level by mid-July. In June, the newspaper was reporting the good news that "the House of Representatives version of the Public Works Administration Bill included an appropriation of approximately $3 million, funds to be used by the U.S. Corps of Engineers to construct recreation areas around the reservoir."

The long days of anticipation seemed worth it now to LaGrange and Troup County residents who were beginning to believe that picnics and camping weekends were soon to come with pavilions, restrooms and many recreational opportunities offered by the lake. Many local residents were either making plans to buy or buying boats of all sizes to be used on the lake for fishing, sailing or just joy riding. Some families were even selecting houseboats.

"The long awaited day of the dedication of the West Point Dam and Powerhouse came on June 7, 1975," as reported in the *Daily News*. This was a big event for all of this area of West Georgia, with national as well as state and local dignitaries on hand. This important milestone marked the beginning of many changes the West Point Dam and Lake would bring to this entire area.

Bringing to a close this "West Point Dam and West Point Lake Review" is an announcement of the construction of the first private marina to serve the area. In September 1975, the newspaper reported, "A Highland Marina and recreational area is being built off the Whitaker Road, near LaGrange; the first private development on the Georgia side of the West Point Reservoir. The first phase, expected to be completed in sixty days, will include roads and boat slips for the wet storage of boats." On its completion in November 1975, the daily reported: "In just a few days, a horde of floating strips will be sailing around Whitaker public service area on the West Point Reservoir looking like the Spanish Armada as 100 slips are installed in the Highland Marina."

As the days were fast approaching for the 1976 bicentennial year to begin, one more event relating to the celebration occurred in November 1975, when the *Daily News* announced, "LaGrange has been declared a 'Bicentennial City,' in spite of the fact that it did not exist in 1776."

"This action was deemed appropriate," the story added, "because the City Council of LaGrange has honored the memory of one of the greatest heroes of American Independence, as well as honoring the Bicentennial of the glorious year of 1776, by voting to adopt an emblem for the city that combines the coat of arms of the Lafayette family with the easily recognized emblem of the original thirteen states."

LaGrange began its formal bicentennial observance in January 1976 with a bang! All the preliminary planning paid off. That first month brought quality reminders of our nation's history and glory. An early January issue of the *Daily News* published a report of what was to come:

> *LaGrange will observe the 200th birthday of the country with a slate of 1976 Bicentennial activities beginning January 15, and scheduled to continue through August. January 15, in Smith Parlor at LaGrange College, Count Rene de Chambrun, great, great grandson of Lafayette, will introduce an exhibit of paintings depicting episodes in the life of General Lafayette by Charles Hargens, a well-known artist and illustrator of historical scenes. Friday, January 16, at Price Theater, on the college campus, Count de Chambrun will deliver an address on Lafayette and will receive an honorary degree of Doctor of Humane Letters from LaGrange College. Later in the day he will place a wreath at the statue of Lafayette in the town Square. The statue will be formally dedicated on February 21.*

The bicentennial wasn't the only newsmaker in the early days of 1976. An action that brought lasting and rewarding results was the formal inauguration of a program of activities for the elderly citizens of the city. The *Daily News* announced in January that a Troup County Senior Center had been established in LaGrange under the Troup County Recreation Commission. The story explained, "The Center is the result of the cooperative efforts of Dixie Mills, the Kiwanis Club, the Junior Service League and the Troup County Council on Aging."

Further details revealed that the center would be located at 200 Dixie Street in a building owned by West Point Pepperell's Dixie Mill. The company had made the property available to the Recreation Commission to be used by elderly citizens. Services available there would include recreational activities such as socials, table games, hobby clubs and other special meetings. The center was to be open five days a week from 9:00 a.m. to 4:00 p.m., operated under volunteer supervision. Three categories of memberships would be: senior citizens—sixty-five years old or older—no charge; individual members—those nearing sixty-five—three dollars per year; and sponsoring members—those merchants and businesses that wish to support the organization—ten dollars per year.

On February 1, 1976, members of the older and younger generations in LaGrange and many county and West Georgia residents attended the dedication and open house for the new LaGrange Memorial Library building, located on the site of the old Harwell Avenue School. According to the *Daily News* report on that occasion, "The library was built at a cost of $710,000, and the building will house the Troup-Harris-Coweta Regional Library."

The story explained, "In July of 1974, a $250,000 grant from the State Board of Education cleared the way to begin building a new library for LaGrange, to replace the old one on Church Street that was no longer adequate in space. Both city and county governments pledged $82,500 initially for the library and Callaway Foundation, Inc. contributed $165,000 to the effort." The decision to make it a regional library came later and increased the amount of territory and services it would cover.

The February coverage of the local bicentennial activities began with a report in the *Daily News* from a spokesman for the First Presbyterian Church announcing that its "church bells will ring each day at noon in an effort to remind the residents of the community of the need for regular prayer for our nation. This will continue through the remainder of this Bicentennial year."

The public was invited to "a fireworks display, by fireworks professionals at Granger Park in LaGrange on the night of February 20, as the kick-off for the local Bicentennial occasions," according to the *Daily News*. One of the most important events in the celebration, plans for which had been announced in details reported earlier, took place as scheduled the following afternoon. A tremendous crowd of patriotic citizens attended this historic event as reported:

> *A major part of the overall celebration of the Bicentennial in LaGrange was held on Saturday, at 3 p.m., on Lafayette Square when the Square, the statue of Lafayette and the fountain were all dedicated. Foreign dignitaries from France, as well as many area residents, were present for the dedications. The Atlanta Symphony Orchestra presented a concert featuring music of the Revolutionary period on Saturday evening, and the public attended at no charge. The concert was sponsored by the LaGrange Bicentennial Commission, and was funded through a grant from the Georgia Commission for the Humanities.*

Five Boy Scouts in a local troop were featured in a front-page story in the *News* in March 1976 as they reached the Eagle Scout rank simultaneously. This event received special attention, as noted: "Yellow Jacket District Scout executive Bob Banks says this is the first time five Scouts in one troop have reached Eagle Scout rank at the same time in the history of this district. It is possibly the first time in the history of the Boy Scouts of America."

"The five boys from Troop 3, sponsored by the Pleasant Grove Methodist Church, were Paul Cooley, Doyle Hagler, Tommy Barber, Wayne Martin and Jody Perdue," the *News* reported.

On April 17, the LaGrange Jaycees sponsored a parade in downtown LaGrange as another activity of the bicentennial observance. The *Daily News* reported, "The theme for the parade was, 'We Love America.'" Many clubs and institutions were represented in the parade, which brought more visibility and greater participation in the nation's 200th anniversary celebration in LaGrange.

The next special bicentennial event covered by the *Daily News* was a gigantic worship service held at night on July 4 at the Callaway Stadium. It was coordinated by the Joint Worship Committee of the Commission, with all churches in the area participating. As Commission Chairman Henry described the gathering, it was "a special service of worship to affirm our faith and rededicate our lives to God, who has made this nation great."

July 4, 1976, also brought a bicentennial announcement of a more personal kind to four very happy families, with a news report in the *Daily News* from the local hospital. It read: "Four 'Bicentennial Babies' were born at the West Georgia Medical Center in LaGrange on the nation's two hundredth birthday, July 4. There wasn't a boy in the bunch. The four little girls are: Valrico LaSheba Beale, the first to arrive; Leslie Suzanne Saxon, Bonnie Magalynna Newell and Jennifer Towles McClellan."

In January 1977, in an editorial, the *Daily News* reminded its readers that "while the Bicentennial celebration was behind them, they should remember "that American Independence wasn't won in 1776, as many people seem to think." It continued:

> *The Declaration of Independence, adopted on July 4, 1776, was a brilliant document. Its adoption was a courageous act. But it did not set a single colonist free. Declaring independence was one thing. Winning it was something else. Thus, it is well to recall that in the bitter winter of 1777–78, a year and a half after the Declaration of Independence, Washington's army huddled in the snow at Valley Forge. Many thought then that the cause of independence was hopeless. Our legacy of liberty was bequeathed not in ink, but in blood. The Continental Army, not the Continental Congress, spelled the difference between freedom and failure.*

Another service to help senior citizens in the area was launched around this time. It was called "The Link" and described as "a communications lifeline for the elderly" by the local daily. The newspaper's announcement explained, "The Link' is a new service being offered to elderly citizens, especially to those living alone, through the Troup County Council on Aging. Its purpose is to provide daily telephone contact with the elderly people in the area who need assistance. The program will be operated by volunteers."

LaGrange residents have become known throughout the state for their efforts to preserve for future generations the best traditions, as well as the most treasured structural reminders of the city's past—at least those that have integrity and are worthy of preservation and restoration. In this decade, the local historical society, established in 1972, began a new project that was reported in the *Daily News*:

> *As one of its projects, the Ocfuskee Historical Society is taking a massive inventory of Troup County's notable houses, buildings and sites, which will be the focus of the society's work in historic preservation in the coming years. Volunteers will aid in the canvass of the properties. The three members of the special committee assigned to this project are Mrs. Jenny Copeland, Mrs. Darlene Hunnicutt and Mrs. Lynne Morgan.*

This was just one of many worthwhile projects sponsored by this society, which was one of the fastest-growing and most active organizations in town. The name of the group was changed in a later decade and remains the Troup County Historical Society.

The society's preservation efforts have been impressive and effective, and its members have also enjoyed the social side. Their costume parties, held annually for many years as fundraisers for the organization's projects, became known for their elegance, entertainment and imaginative themes. The *Daily News* account of the party held in October 1977 offers a description of one gathering of the group:

> *Hollywood figures from the past and present came to life Friday night as the Ocfuskee Historical Society staged its annual costume party at the Highland Country Club. The theme, "Hooray for Hollywood," brought out the ham in dozens of local citizens. And then there was the staid group, who had "extra" or "director" on their name tags. The only authentic looking one in this group was Seale Hipp, who did a good take-off on*

LaGrange National Bank, built in 1917. The building was renovated by Callaway Foundation, Inc., as a gift to the Troup County Historical Society for offices and archives in 1982.

*Cecil B. DeMille. Some of the characters were Phyliss Diller, alias Liz Rakestraw; Eleanor Roosevelt (Mrs. James Holder); Wonder Woman (Taylor Merrill); and a "man in a white coat who carried a lethal looking over-sized hypodermic needle" (Tom Woosley). Then there was a dapper-looking little Charlie Chaplin (Peggy Woosley); Hawkeye from the TV Mash series (Dr. Bob Copeland); Aunt Pittypat (Mrs. Mary Jane Crayton); Peter Pan (Lura Edge); Wendy and John (Mr. and Mrs. Ned Daniel); Cowboys (Charles Hudson and Charles Foster); Prince Rainier and Grace Kelly (Mr. and Mrs. Dan Durand); and Prissy and Scarlett O'Hara (Mr. and Mrs. Frank Luton).*

From the earliest years of the 1970s to the end of the decade, there was evidence of the concern and affection the LaGrange and Troup County planners and authorities felt for the older generation of their citizens. Some of these examples have been reported earlier.

A new service, still contributing today to the quality of life of older citizens, was reported in 1977 when the Troup County Senior Center launched a "Hot Lunch Program" on weekdays that offered inexpensive luncheon meals for the elders, as well as more daily recreational programs for them.

Concern for the older citizens did not mean that the planners and authorities were forgetting the needs of the younger adults. Two important programs for them were announced in the *Daily News* in 1979.

The Troup Area Technical and Vocational School expanded its facilities and its area of instructions, and LaGrange College began a master's degree program in business administration to make it possible for young business executives employed locally to get a further business degree at home.

These new programs served as reminders that earlier in this decade, in 1973, the local college had instituted a master's program in education so that local teachers, as well as the college's regular students, could continue their education and get a further degree in that field in LaGrange. An associate degree in nursing had also been added at the college in 1973 for local women wanting further education to help in their careers in nursing, as well as for traditional students on campus. In 1974, the college had reactivated its night classes. All of these additions that benefited local adults as well as the regular college-age students were reported in the *Daily News* as they were occurring.

It seems appropriate to end the decade of the 1970s with the subject of education, since it began that way. Reporting school and college news, of individuals and institutions, has always been a priority for the *LaGrange Daily News*, as it was for our earliest local newspapers. Many time-worn clippings from newspaper pages can be found in scrapbooks made by students who attended LaGrange schools and colleges through the years.

## MOSAIC MUSINGS FROM THE 1970S

*With the voter apathy across the nation, Mrs. Clementine Higgins of LaGrange, who will be 95-years-old next month, could hardly wait to cast her ballot this morning in the Democratic Primary Run-off Election. Shortly after 8 a.m., she was at the National Guard Armory to mark her ballot.*

*The chimes that you heard for the first time today* [September 1976], *are coming from the Schulmerich Carillon which has recently been installed at St. Mark's Episcopal Church in memory of Miss Jean Swank, given in a bequest from her father, the late Roy C. Swank. St. Mark's is the only church in LaGrange to have a carillon at this time.*

*There is going to be some pistol-packing in LaGrange, Troup County and Georgia, but local law enforcement officials are not worried as long as it is done legally. So far, 115 people in Troup County have applied for the State's new license to carry an unlimited number of concealed weapons. It takes twenty to thirty days to process the application, including an investigation to make certain no one has committed a felony within the last ten years, or a forcible misdemeanor (such as assault) within the last five years. No one in the last two cases is granted a license to conceal a weapon. Under present Georgia law, a person can have a handgun at his home, business or in his car without a license, but it cannot be in public without a license. This is not affected by the new law.*

## OPENINGS/FOUNDINGS

LaGrange Academy (private school), 1970; Downtown Development Authority, 1972; Ocfuskee Historical Society (renamed Troup County Historical Society), 1972; Industrial Development Authority of LaGrange, 1973; Division of Nursing at LaGrange College, 1973; LaGrange Junior Service League, 1973; West Georgia Medical Center (formerly City-County Hospital) opened new six-story building, 1974; new LaGrange Memorial Library Building, 1974; last leg of I-85 in Troup County, 1977; Chattahoochee Valley Art Association Museum, located in 1892 Troup County Jail building, 1978; I-185 opened, 1979

## HAPPENINGS

City of Hogansville celebrates centennial, 1970; integration of all public schools in LaGrange and Troup County, 1970; county manager position created for Troup County, 1974; dedication of new Elm City Lodge, 1974; West Point Dam dedicated, 1975; Bellevue, historic home of Confederate senator Benjamin Harvey Hill, declared national landmark by U.S. Park

Bellevue, LaGrange Woman's Club headquarters. The building underwent a complete restoration in 1975 as a gift of Callaway Foundation, Inc. *Bill Holt, photographer.*

Service, 1976; LaGrange celebrated nation's bicentennial, 1976; dedication of statue of Lafayette on Lafayette Square in LaGrange, 1976; dedication of new Shrine Club, 1977; prime minister of New Zealand visited LaGrange, 1977

# 1970s Decade Review—Nationally

Space exploration by Apollo 14 and 15, 1971; nation mourned death of Harry S. Truman, thirty-third president of the United States, 1972; Apollo astronauts land on moon for more exploration, 1972; ground troops withdrawn from Vietnam by United States, 1973; *Roe v. Wade* Supreme Court decision made abortions legal, 1973; President Richard M. Nixon resigned after Watergate scandal, pardoned by new president, Gerald Ford, 1974; official beginning of bicentennial observance of our nation's independence, March 1, 1975; former Georgia governor James Earl Carter elected president of United States, 1976; personal computers marketed, 1977; nation mourned death of Elvis Presley, 1977; mandatory U.S. retirement age raised from sixty-five to seventy, 1978; cigarette smoking linked to cancer, heart and lung diseases by U.S. surgeon general, 1979

# WINSOME MURMURS FROM THE 1970S

*With tombstones for a background, a LaGrange couple said their wedding vows Tuesday afternoon in the old Confederate Cemetery off Miller Street. The two were married under spreading cedar trees amid the gravestones of fallen Civil War soldiers. The young groom said he and his bride decided to marry there because "a lot of good marriages have ended in the cemetery. We wanted a good one to start here."*

*A New Year's Eve party at a local night club was in the dark for a while Wednesday night, when someone stole the electricity. The owner of the Rock Garden, on Whitesville Road, reported to police that someone stole two electric meters, outside of the place, which were supplying the electricity to the club. The meters were taken while the party was in full swing. The club was plunged into darkness, but those inside enjoyed dancing in the dark. A vandalism report was filed by the police.*

*It's Leap Year, Ladies! Only once every four years...and this is it! Eligible bachelors in LaGrange who meet a lass with a certain twinkle of marriage in her eye had better be more wary than ever this year because girls have the privilege of doing the proposing during leap year. 1976 may be the Centennial Year, but it is also Leap Year, and that comes only once every four years. Custom has it that the privilege, of allowing women to do the proposing in a leap year, is traced to an old story about St. Patrick and St. Bridget. Bridget went to Patrick in tears because there was unrest among the women because of the unfair custom that prevented women from taking the initiative in matrimony. Patrick was sympathetic to the women's grief and finally agreed to give the women one out of every four years—and the longest one at that.*

*You've heard of the womanless wedding before, but this one may take the cake—including the wedding cake. The LaGrange Academy will sponsor a womanless wedding at the Callaway Auditorium on February 19, as a fund-raiser for the new private school. Attorney James Weldon will play the part of the groom, with Dr. James Doerr as the shy bride. Their stage names are "Jamie Welldone" and "Dainty Dumbetta." John Wyatt and Jim Killebrew will be the mother and father of the groom, with Dr. George McCrary and Bill Baker as father and mother of the bride. Pete Bittick, Emmett Fling, William Hudson and Nick Woodson will be flower girls. Ushers will be Ed Madan and Pat Hunnicutt. Master of Ceremonies for the event will be Philip Cleaveland and Mrs. LeMerle Perdue will be director.*

*Graffiti: Today's dollar is built for speed, not endurance.*

*Graffiti: Today you can be on the cover of "Time" magazine one week, and start serving it the next.*

# Epilogue

Every month from December 1993 through December 2010, "Memoried Glances" has brought to its readers in the *LaGrange Daily News* the news items and commentary from the past (1894 to 1979), reprinted here in *Remembering LaGrange*. The author is grateful to her readers, to the newspaper, to Jessica Berzon and Hilary McCullough, The History Press and to all who have assisted her in this effort to present her research in another genre.

This book concludes with the end of the decade of the 1970s in LaGrange instead of proceeding into the middle of the 1980s, already researched and covered in more recently published columns. We did not want the book to end in the middle of a decade.

It seems appropriate now to observe that the people who knew the importance of religion and education, and who appreciated the "good things" of life when LaGrange was established in 1828, have been followed by generations who have appreciated the legacy the earlier residents left for us to enjoy. Their descendants in each generation have wanted to continue passing this legacy on to those who followed them. As citizens of LaGrange today, we are still being blessed and inspired by their example.

The weekly and daily newspapers, published in LaGrange through the years, have contributed to and are part of this legacy. They have preserved for us local, state, national and world history day by day or week by week, as it happened. Without copies of these newspapers that were available for research, this book would have been impossible.

My prayer is that there will always be a newspaper in LaGrange to continue reporting and offering commentary on the news that records the history of the times and the lives of people who are blessed by living in the greatest place in the world—my hometown—LaGrange, Troup County, Georgia.

# Appendix
# The Editors

In a sincere attempt to give attribution to the editors of the newspapers researched by decades for this book, your writer regrets that often the masthead did not include a designated editor's name. In some cases, no names were given; in others, the publisher's name was the only one listed. For this reason, it was impossible to credit, with any certainty, the writer of specific editorials because they were not signed.

If an editor's name did appear on the masthead, it will be given in our attributions by decade. If not, the publisher(s) name will be given, if on the masthead. This book uses the attribution for editorship provided by the newspaper ownership on the masthead.

Having been part of a weekly newspaper operation for ten years of her life, this writer knows that newspaper production, whether weekly or daily, is a team effort. News ink gets in your blood. Wanting credit for what you wrote is not the important thing. The goal, every week, or every day, is "getting the paper out" and into the hands of the readers. Perhaps that is why we see so few signed editorials. Hometown newspaper editors are traditionally "team players."

*LaGrange Reporter*, from 1894
1894–March 1896—S. Pope Callaway, Editor & Proprietor (d. March 17)
1896–June 1901—James P. Callaway, Editor; Mrs. S. Pope Callaway, Publisher
June 1901–March 1902—W.W. Randall, Editor; Mrs. S. Pope Callaway, Publisher

March 1902–1904—George E. Billinghurst, Editor; Fuller E. Callaway, Proprietor

1904–1912—J.O. Bell, Editor & Publisher

February 1912–March 1912—L.H. Jenkins, Editor

March 1912–unknown date—J.A. Perry, Editor & Publisher

1919—John H. Jones, Editor

1927—H.R. Emory, Editor

*LaGrange Graphic*

1918–1922—S.G.Woodall, Editor

1923–1928—W.A. Richardson, Editor

1929 (January, February, March)—Robert Ware, Editor

April 1929—merged into *Graphic-Shuttle*

June 21, 1929—consolidation of all three newspapers, *LaGrange News* and *Graphic-Shuttle*

*LaGrange Daily News*

1930–1934—merger of *LaGrange Daily News*, *LaGrange Reporter* and *LaGrange Graphic-Shuttle*—Roy C. Swank, General Manager for General Newspapers, Inc.

1934–1961—Roy C. Swank, Publisher; in the mid-1940s to mid-1950s, a co-publisher, Helen P. Swank (managing/city editor positions during this time held by Don Downs, James Wood and Phil Harrison)

1961–1979—Glen O. Long, Publisher (Long served as editor, with editorial assistance by C. Lee West)

This information provided by newspaper mastheads in years covered in research for this book.

# About the Author

Julia Traylor Dyar is a fifth-generation resident of Troup County, Georgia. She received a bachelor of arts degree in French from LaGrange College in 1946.

After her marriage to the youngest weekly newspaper editor in Georgia, the late Hubert Lenhardt Dyar, in 1948, she began writing a weekly column and was associate editor of the *Royston (Georgia) Record* for ten years. The couple moved to Atlanta, where she was assistant manager and later manager of Georgia Press Association, the trade association of the state's weekly and daily newspapers, until 1978. She was voted a life member of the GPA at that time.

Mrs. Dyar returned to her hometown, LaGrange, Georgia, to be public relations director for her alma mater, LaGrange College, for almost fifteen years, before her retirement in 1993. Since then, she has written a weekly historical column, "Memoried Glances," for the *LaGrange Daily News*.

She is a member of LaGrange's First Baptist Church on the Square, where she teaches an adult women's Sunday school class and is chairman of the church's Archives/History Committee. She is a member of the LaGrange Historic Preservation Commission, a municipal appointment, and is a member and a past president of the Troup County Historical Society.

A compulsive reader, she is a member and a past president of the Round Table, LaGrange's oldest book club, founded in 1931.

Her claim to fame is being an aunt, great-aunt and great-great-aunt.

# The Cover

The art for the cover of *Remembering LaGrange* includes four postcard images, used courtesy of Chris Cleaveland from his vintage postcard collection. They are a 1920s Main Street scene, McLendon's Pond, the Callaway Tower and Smith Hall at LaGrange College, all of which appear with captions in this book.

Also pictured is a partial view of a *LaGrange Daily News* color photograph (back cover, upper left) of a mural of historical downtown locations and events, painted on a wall next to the LaGrange–Troup County Chamber of Commerce Plaza on Lafayette Square. The mural was painted by Wes Hardin, a well-known Alabama artist who has created murals throughout the Southeast and in Washington, D.C. The photograph is used courtesy of the *LaGrange Daily News* and the Downtown LaGrange Development Authority. The Authority was a sponsor of the mural project, which was funded by a grant from the City of LaGrange and other gifts.

The central image of the mural, shown at left on the back cover, is the 1904 Troup County Courthouse, located on the square in LaGrange until it burned in 1936. Other images are, *from left*, the "Unforgettable" Newell's Hat Shop, circa 1933, in business on the square from 1931 to 1977, background here for a smiling Franklin D. Roosevelt, often seen in downtown LaGrange during his frequent visits to Warm Springs; the LaGrange City Hall, opened in 1927 and still in use today; and a half-image of the Blue Goose Café, circa 1960, a popular business in downtown LaGrange.